# THE RISE OF A NEW MEDIA BARON AND THE EMERGING THREAT OF NEWS DESERTS

By Penelope Muse Abernathy,
Knight Chair in Journalism and Digital Media Economics

The Center for Innovation and Sustainability in Local Media

School of Media and Journalism

University of North Carolina at Chapel Hill

ISBN 978-1-4696-3402-9 (pbk.: alk. paper)
ISBN 978-1-4696-3403-6 (ebook)


Distributed by the University of North Carolina Press
116 South Boundary Street
Chapel Hill, NC 27514-3808
www.uncpress.org

# CONTENTS

Much attention has been focused in recent years on the country's largest and most revered national newspapers as they struggle to adapt to the digital age. This report focuses, instead, on the thousands of other papers in this country that cover the news of its small towns, city neighborhoods, booming suburbs and large metropolitan areas.

The journalists on these papers often toil without recognition outside their own communities. But the stories their papers publish can have an outsized impact on the decisions made by residents in those communities, and, ultimately, on the quality of their lives. By some estimates, community newspapers provide as much as 85 percent of "the news that feeds democracy" at the state and local levels.[1] This means the fates of newspapers and communities are inherently linked. If one fails, the other suffers. Therefore, it matters who owns the local newspaper because the decisions owners make affect the health and vitality of the community.

For the past two years, the School of Media and Journalism at the University of North Carolina at Chapel Hill has collected, researched and analyzed data from 2004 to 2016 on more than 9,500 local newspapers. Our 2016 database includes1,700 small weeklies with a circulation of 2,000 or less, as well as 20 large metro dailies with more than 200,000 weekday circulation, such as the Chicago Tribune and Washington Post. However, because our focus is on traditional local newspapers, regardless of their size, we excluded the large national papers—The New York Times, Wall Street Journal and USA Today—from our analysis, as well as specialty publications such as business journals and shoppers.

This report, divided into four sections, documents dramatic changes over the past decade. With the industry in distress, local newspapers are shrinking, and some are vanishing. At the same time, a new type of newspaper owner has emerged, very different from traditional publishers, the best of whom sought to balance business interests with civic responsibility to the community where their paper was located. As newspapers confront an uncertain future, the choices these new owners make could determine whether vast "news deserts" arise in communities and regions throughout the country. This has implications not just for the communities where these papers are located, but also, in the long-term, for all of America.

Over the past decade, a new media baron has emerged in the United States. Private equity funds, hedge funds and other newly formed investment partnerships have swooped in to buy—and actively manage—newspapers all over the country. These new owners are very different from the newspaper publishers that preceded them. For the most part they lack journalism experience or the sense of civic mission traditionally embraced by publishers and editors. Newspapers represent only a fraction of their vast business portfolios—ranging from golf courses to subprime lenders—worth hundreds of millions, even billions, of dollars. Their mission is to make money for their investors, so they operate with a short-term, earnings-first focus and are prepared to get rid of any holdings—including newspapers—that fail to produce what they judge to be an adequate profit.

The rise of this new media baron coincides with a period of immense disruption and distress for the entire newspaper industry. With profits and readership declining dramatically, every newspaper publisher is grappling with an uncertain future, and many worry about their paper's long-term survival. As a result of these dynamics, many smaller cities and towns could lose their local newspapers and with them the reliable news and information essential to a community's economy, governance and quality of life. The prospect of such "news deserts" across entire regions of the country would have significant long-term political, social and economic consequences.

Within the last decade, several hundred newspapers have shut down, merged or cut back from daily to weekly publication. Most of the approximately 8,000 local newspapers that survive are small dailies and weeklies with a circulation of less than 15,000. Many are the primary, if not sole, source of local news.[2] The decisions that the new, as well as long-time, owners of newspapers make in the near future will have implications both for the health of local journalism and for the vitality of their communities. This report documents and analyzes dramatic ownership trends during a pivotal decade and considers the long-term implications. Here are some of the findings:

• Since 2004, more than a third of the country's newspapers have changed ownership; some sold two or more times. Faced with steep declines in revenue, many long-time owners have declared bankruptcy or decided to sell while they can. Since the cost of acquiring a newspaper has fallen in tandem with shrinking profits, astute buyers with access to financing have snapped up newspapers at bargain rates in small and mid-sized markets. The new owners can then cut costs and recoup their investment in only a few short years. Whole newspaper chains have disappeared, acquired by other companies. Before the 2008–09 Great Recession, the most active acquirers were large publicly traded chains, such as Lee, McClatchy and News Corp. Since then, newly formed investment groups, including New Media/GateHouse, Digital First and Civitas, have been the most aggressive purchasers.

The largest newspaper companies are larger than ever, and still growing. Big chains can achieve significant cost savings by merging production, sales and editorial functions of several newspapers, while also amassing an audience large enough to remain attractive to advertisers. At the end of 2004, the three largest companies owned 487 newspapers with a combined circulation of 9.8 million. Today, the three largest companies own about 900 papers that have a combined circulation of 12.7 million.

The large investment groups tend to employ a standard formula in managing their newspapers — aggressive cost cutting paired with revenue increases and financial restructuring, including bankruptcy. Most have financed acquisitions with significant debt. To reduce costs, the new media barons have typically laid off staff, frozen wages, reduced benefits and consolidated sales and editorial functions. With revenues and profits still declining, much initial cost cutting has been painful, but necessary — and may have actually saved some newspapers in the short term. However, for the most part, profits derived from cost cutting have not been reinvested to improve their newspapers' journalism, but used instead to pay loans, management fees and shareholder dividends.

In contrast to 20th century media companies that would "buy and hold" newspapers for many years, the new newspaper-owning investment groups actively manage their properties, keeping a short-term focus on the bottom line. Because the media barons acquire newspapers primarily — or solely — as an investment, often as a relatively modest part of a diverse portfolio of nonmedia assets, they do not, or need not, pay close attention to the quality of journalism produced by their newspapers. They are constantly buying, trading and selling newspapers in their portfolio. Because they own so many newspapers, they can absorb the loss if an individual newspaper fails. If investment firms cannot sell an underperforming newspaper, they close it, leaving communities without a newspaper or any other reliable source of local news and information.

Investment groups are geographically concentrated. They own between a fifth and a third of the newspapers in many states in New England, the upper Midwest, and the South. The seven largest investment groups own and operate more than 1,000 newspapers in 42 states, or close to 15 percent of all American newspapers, as defined for this study. Five of the seven largest newspaper-owning investment firms did not exist a decade ago, so it is difficult to predict whether they will continue to acquire papers or decide to sell the newspapers they currently own and move onto other more attractive investment options.

Most newspapers owned and operated by investment groups are located in economically struggling small and mid-sized communities where the newspaper is the only source of local news. Without significant fresh investment, the bond between newspapers and their readers and advertisers will erode. Strong newspapers enhance the quality of life by producing journalism that documents a community's life and identifies its issues, while providing advertising that connects consumers with local businesses.

Newspapers must adapt to the digital age to remain viable community builders, or else they remain tethered to the fast-fading print-only world of yesterday. This will require a significant investment by newspaper owners and a long-term commitment to these struggling communities, not the short-term focus on earnings that has, so far, been the hallmark of the investment groups that have aggressively purchased papers in the last decade. Some communities have already become news deserts, having lost their local newspapers. Many others may soon follow.

Concerns about the role and ownership of newspapers have been voiced and debated since the founding of the country. However, the dramatic shift in ownership of newspapers over the past decade — coupled with the rapidly deteriorating finances of community papers — brings added urgency to a new version of an age-old question: In the digital age, what is the civic responsibility of newspaper owners to their communities?

"A newspaper is an institution developed by modern civilization to present the news of the day, to foster commerce and industry, to inform and lead public opinion, and to furnish that check upon government which no constitution has ever been able to provide," proclaimed Robert R. McCormick, publisher of the Chicago Tribune from 1925 to 1955.

For two centuries, newspapers have been an indispensable auditor of democracy at all levels in this county.  By documenting the shifting landscape of newspaper ownership and assessing the threat of news deserts, this report seeks to raise awareness that universities, for-profit and nonprofit organizations, community activists and government may have greater roles to play in addressing the challenges confronting local news media and our democracy.

What can be done to save the journalism that has been provided by community newspapers for more than 200 years? There are no simple answers and no guarantees. It will take a concerted and committed effort by many to avert a growing number of news deserts.

# A DRAMATICALLY CHANGED LANDSCAPE

## FEWER NEWSPAPERS, FEWER READERS, FEWER OWNERS

The years between 2004 and 2014 were pivotal for the newspaper industry, reversing the good fortune of the previous decade when advertising revenue and profits spiked, while circulation declined very slowly.

By 2004, it was apparent to industry analysts and investors that the migration of readers and advertisers to the internet threatened the soundness of the century-old newspaper business model. But few predicted how quickly that pace would pick up and profitability would decline. Then, the Great Recession of 2008–2009 delivered a staggering blow to advertising and the bottom line, driving many owners out of business and giving rise to a new kind of media baron.

The surviving newspapers and their owners confront a significantly different business environment today than in 2004. This report analyzes data on more than 9,500 daily and weekly papers at three intervals between the end of 2004 through mid-2016 to document how dramatically the industry has changed in recent years. Updated through July 30, 2016, it draws on statistics in the 2004 and 2014 Editor & Publisher's *Newspaper Data Book* and 2016 E&P data accessed online, as well as information shared by the consulting firm BIA/Kelsey.[i] Faculty and researchers in the University of North Carolina at Chapel Hill School of Media and Journalism supplemented the information in these two databases with extensive reporting and research. They conducted interviews with industry analysts and professionals, and analyzed U.S. Census data, as well as the financial records and press releases issued by newspaper owners.

This analysis shows that the pace of change in the industry is accelerating, even as the underlying economics of ink-on-paper continue to worsen.

---

[1]  BIA/Kelsey conducted a telephone survey of newspaper executives and managers while Editor & Publisher employed a digital and mail survey of senior executives at individual papers. Both relied on the accurate feedback of respondents and have the type of reporting errors inherent in any survey. When we spotted errors, we corrected them in our database and will continue to update our analysis as new information becomes available. If you detect an error, please fill out and submit the "corrections" form available on our website, www.newspaperownership.com.

How many newspapers are there in U.S. today? It depends on how they are counted. The number of newspapers listed in various databases ranges from 7,000 to more than 12,000. Industry spokesmen and analysts estimate there are 11,000 newspapers.

The focus of this report is on local newspapers that publish journalism oriented toward a specific geographic region, community or ethnic group. Therefore, national newspapers, specialty publications—such as business journals and lifestyle magazines—and shoppers or similar advertisement-based printed materials were excluded from the UNC database and this analysis.
ii

After these adjustments, there were 8,591 local newspapers published at least once a week listed in the 2004 UNC database.

Between 2004 and 2014, 664 newspapers vanished from UNC's database. At the end of 2014, only 7,927 local papers were still being published. This total included large daily metros, such as the Los Angeles Times, as well as very small weeklies and dailies. Of the surviving papers in 2014, the vast majority—6,474—had circulation of less than 15,000.

### DAILY NEWSPAPERS
In 2014, there were at least 138 fewer daily papers than in 2004. This compared with a loss of 91 in the preceding decade.[3]

Between 2004 and 2014, 42 dailies in 21 states in the UNC database either ceased publication or merged with another paper. Since 2014, an additional 11 dailies have closed or merged. Eight of the closed papers since 2004 were in a metro area, such as Denver, Honolulu and Seattle, where there was more than one daily, usually published

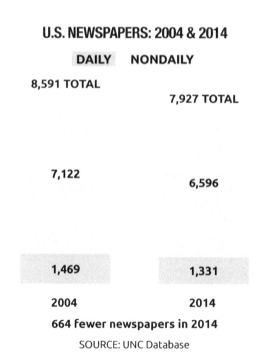

**U.S. NEWSPAPERS: 2004 & 2014**

DAILY   NONDAILY

8,591 TOTAL

7,927 TOTAL

7,122            6,596

1,469            1,331

2004            2014

**664 fewer newspapers in 2014**

SOURCE: UNC Database

under a joint operating agreement with another company.[4] But most of the other 22 papers that closed were the last surviving dailies in their communities. This included the 188-year-old Daily Southerner, covering the eastern North Carolina community of Tarboro, population 11,000, and the 111-year-old Medina Journal-Register, covering that village of about 6,000 on the Erie Canal in upstate New York. In 2013, the Journal-Register, with 1,500 circulation, cut back publication from daily to three times a week in an attempt to stave off closure. Both papers closed in 2014. (See newspaperownership.com/additional-material/ for a list of closed or merged dailies from 2004-2016.)

More than 100 newspapers in the database shifted from daily to "weekly" or nondaily delivery of their print editions. This study, as does Editor & Publisher, defines "weekly" as three or fewer times a week. All but 90 of those reconstituted nondaily papers had a circulation of less than 10,000. Five of the six largest newspapers to

---

ii   The three national papers excluded from the database are *The New York Times, Wall Street Journal* and *USA Today.* In addition to shoppers and specialty publications, newspapers published less frequently than once a week were also excluded. As a result, some statistics in this report may differ from those listed on company websites. Even so, our adjusted total may be overstating the number of local newspapers, since many companies list geographic editions and supplements as separate papers.

## THE VANISHING DAILY NEWSPAPER: 2004–2016

CLOSED/MERGED    REDUCED TO WEEKLY

Between 2004 and 2016, fifty-six dailies closed or merged; 109 shifted to nondaily publication.

SOURCE: UNC Database

See newspaperownership.com/changed-landscape/ for location of daily papers that were closed or merged, or shifted to nondaily publication.

scale back print publication to three times a week were owned by Advance, which moved in 2011 to emphasize its online newspaper sites.[5]

The significant cost of publishing daily print editions is likely to accelerate the trend to nondaily distribution in the coming decade. Only two nondailies shifted to daily distribution—small papers in Texas (clantonadvertiser.com) and Alabama (dailytrib.com), each with less than 7,000 circulation.

A handful of newspaper owners tried to defy the odds and launch a daily newspaper, but only one was still operating in 2016. The owner of a local Christian television station launched a second daily paper with a circulation of 3,000 in Kittanning, PA, in 2008 (kittanningpaper.com). In contrast, the Long Beach, California, Register, started in 2013, and the Los Angeles Register, in 2014, were both shut down after only several months of operation.[6]

### WEEKLY AND NONDAILY NEWSPAPERS

The economics of weeklies and nondailies held up better than for dailies. Between 2004 and 2014, there was a net loss of 526 nondailies in the UNC database. While 1,561 nondailies were discontinued, 1,035 were added, including more than 100 dailies that converted to weekly. Most of the weeklies that closed were suburban editions of daily papers that were merged back into the larger metro paper.

The majority of the "new" weeklies were also in the suburbs. Many were sections in daily papers that were spun out as separate editions. Increasingly, large media companies have been building networks of weeklies in suburban communities, in an attempt to put together a sizable audience that attracts advertisers back to print. For example, by 2014 two companies—Tribune Publishing and Shaw Media—produced and distributed almost all the weeklies in the suburbs of Chicago.

Since 2011, more people have read news online than in a print newspaper, according to the Pew Research Center.[7] So it is not surprising that newspaper circulation plummeted 20 percent between 2004 and 2014.

The dramatic circulation drop occurred despite new rules and guidelines adopted by the industry after 2004 that allowed newspapers to count print and online readership that had been previously excluded.[8] Circulation statistics in the UNC database primarily represent audited print-copy distribution, an admittedly imperfect measure since it does not count the increasing number of people who access local news online. However, readership data for most digital editions of the newspapers in this report are not widely available or comparable. Therefore, print circulation becomes a proxy—albeit imperfect—for the decline in influence and reach of local newspapers.

About half of the decline in circulation stemmed from existing newspapers shedding readers, while the other half resulted from the closing of daily and nondaily newspapers. Daily circulation declined by 28 percent by 2014. Daily newspapers with more than 100,000 in circulation in 2004 suffered a stunning loss of 43 percent. By 2014, only 69 dailies had print circulation above 100,000, down from 102 in 2004.

Circulation of weeklies dropped 15 percent. Larger nondailies with circulation over 50,000 dropped slightly more.

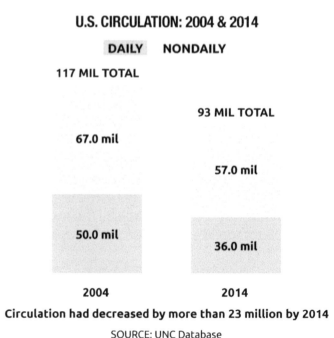

**U.S. CIRCULATION: 2004 & 2014**

**DAILY**    NONDAILY

117 MIL TOTAL

93 MIL TOTAL

67.0 mil

57.0 mil

50.0 mil

36.0 mil

2004

2014

**Circulation had decreased by more than 23 million by 2014**

SOURCE: UNC Database

As economic conditions worsened after 2004, a steady stream of owners decided to sell or declare bankruptcy. More than a third of newspapers changed ownership. Many independent family-owned newspapers were sold to the large chains. As a result, in 2014, the nation had 3,034 newspaper owners, down from 3,897 in 2004.

As the number of owners decreased, consolidation—especially among the largest companies—accelerated. By 2014, the largest 25 companies owned 2,199 papers. The next largest 25 companies owned only 631 papers.

The largest 25 companies in 2014 owned more than half of all dailies in the country—721 out of 1,331—and one-fifth of all nondailies—1,478 out of 6,596.

During the past decade, there has been extensive turnover among the largest owners. Several of the large chains in 2004 were acquired by other companies; others sold divisions or groups of newspapers.

Each of the largest 25 companies in 2004 and 2014 was assessed on the basis of its corporate and financial characteristics and categorized in one of three ways:
- A traditional private chain, such as Hearst or Advance.
- A publicly traded company, such as Gannett or McClatchy.
- An investment entity, in which the principal owners and/or operators are hedge and pension funds, or private and publicly traded equity firms.

### NEWSPAPERS OWNED BY 25 LARGEST COMPANIES: 2004 & 2014

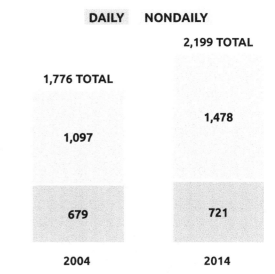

The largest companies owned 423 more papers in 2014

SOURCE: UNC Database

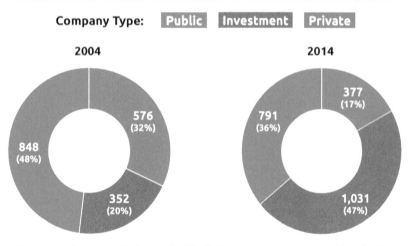

## NEWSPAPERS OWNED BY LARGEST 25 COMPANIES: 2004 & 2014

Company Type: **Public** **Investment** **Private**

**2004**

848 (48%)
576 (32%)
352 (20%)

**2014**

377 (17%)
791 (36%)
1,031 (47%)

**By 2014, investment companies owned almost half of the newspapers owned by the largest 25 companies**

SOURCE: UNC Database

In 2004, the largest 25 companies owned 1,776 papers. The publicly traded companies and private chains owned 80 percent of these papers. Investment entities owned only 20 percent.

By 2014, the largest public and private chains in the country possessed only slightly more than 50 percent of the 2,199 papers now owned by the largest 25 companies. Seven large investment entities — five of which had not existed in 2004 — owned the other half. The next chapter, "The Rise of New Media Baron," documents how and why investment entities have assembled large chains of newspapers in recent years, growing to such prominence in the industry.

Speaking at a worldwide gathering of newspaper editors in 2005, News Corp. Chairman and CEO Rupert Murdoch noted downward readership trends and predicted somewhat facetiously that the "the last reader recycles the last newspaper in 2040."[9] The newspaper world has contracted significantly since that prediction was made.

In 2010, in the wake of the Great Recession, newspaper advertising revenue fell below 1950 levels, adjusted for inflation. It has continued to decline every year since.[10] Today there are many fewer readers, fewer newspapers and fewer owners than a mere decade ago. These dramatic changes, coupled with rapidly deteriorating economics, raise questions about the long-term future of ink-on-paper newspapers and pose difficult choices for the owners of surviving papers.

# THE RISE OF A
# NEW MEDIA BARON

As profits and readership declined rapidly over the past decade, causing immense disruption in the industry, newspaper empires built in the 20th century fell, and a new type of newspaper owner rose to power.

Some of the largest newspaper companies today did not exist in 2004. Private equity funds, pension funds and other investment partnerships have moved quickly to acquire hundreds of distressed papers. They've purchased entire chains that have been forced into bankruptcy, as well as smaller private newspaper companies whose longtime owners have given up struggling to adapt economically and technologically to the digital era.

Today, seven of the largest 25 newspaper owners[iii] are investment groups. Their recently established empires are surpassing in size the large chains of the 20th century, and they are still growing as they continue to snap up more and more ink-on-paper newspapers at bargain prices while disposing of unprofitable ones. Unlike the local owners of the past who had a stake in their communities, or the professional managers who ran those large 20th century chains, these new newspaper owners focus almost exclusively on driving the performance of their holdings, of which newspapers are often a small and expendable part. The decisions that these new newspaper owners make and the business strategies they pursue over the next few years will determine whether these newspapers survive and in what form.

---

[iii] "Largest" is determined by number of newspapers owned, not total circulation.

Over the past century, there have been three types of newspaper owners. The founders, who established iconic newspaper brands such as The New York Times or the Chicago Tribune, dominated the industry in the first half of the 20th century. They were succeeded by corporate newspaper managers in the second half of the century who built large chains, including Gannett and Knight Ridder. Now, in the last decade, investment entities, run by financial portfolio managers, have quickly assembled newspaper groups that dwarf the big chains of the 20th century.

Newspapers in this country are equal parts business enterprises and civic institutions with special constitutional protections. With each generation of newspaper owner, there has been debate about how to prioritize obligations to the public versus those to major shareholders. The newest generation of media barons—the investment portfolio managers—are not journalists nor do they share journalism's traditional civic mission. Their priority is maximizing the return on the assets in their diverse portfolios. Therefore, their rapid ascent raises new and pressing concerns about the responsibilities of newspaper owners in the digital age.

A technological innovation in the 19th century, the steam-powered printing press, gave rise to the first generation of newspaper barons. It allowed newspapers to print and distribute their newspapers to mass audiences, which, in turn, attracted the attention and dollars of advertisers who paid to reach these readers. In the era before radio and television, many newspaper barons amassed great wealth and often wielded tremendous political influence. William Randolph Hearst and Joseph Pulitzer, competing in the era of "yellow journalism," famously used their big-city newspapers to inflame passions leading up to the Spanish-American War.

However, in towns and cities across the country, newspapers were largely owned by local residents. These publishers and their editors often had political clout in their states and cities, but—whether conservative or liberal—they had cultural and economic constraints. If they did not serve the interests of their readers and advertisers, they risked losing business to a competing paper. So, in contrast to the "yellow journalists" of their time, owners such as the Ochs family, which owned the Chattanooga

Times and then The New York Times, or the Bingham family, which owned the Louisville Courier-Journal, worked to establish a reputation for editorial excellence and fairness. In the process, these early newspaper barons established the modern, multi-subject newspaper and became the dominant advertising option for most local businesses.

As radio began to draw audiences and advertising in the 1920s, some of these owners concluded they needed to own more than one or two newspapers to remain competitive with both readers and advertisers. E.W. Scripps and Hearst assembled the first large privately owned "chains," consisting of 20 or more papers in cities across the country.[11] Concerns were immediately voiced about the span and influence of these new chains, but they faded as radio and television began to amass even greater audiences. By 1960, 32 percent of newspapers were owned by a chain, and the early potent media barons had been replaced by a second generation of owners.[12]

Professional managers held most of the executive positions in the large newspaper chains that arose in the latter half of the 20th century. But, in contrast to many other corporations, the newspaper business remained largely a family-centered enterprise. The large chains bore the name of the founders—Gannett, Lee, Knight Ridder, Dow Jones—or the name of the flagship paper—Advance, The New York Times, the Tribune. Often, descendants of the founder held the top posts of publisher, editor, CEO or chairman.

Between 1960 and 1990, another trend emerged: One after another competing paper in communities across the country ceased publication. In an effort to preserve "diverse" viewpoints in major metro areas and save the surviving newspapers, the Department of Justice often approved joint operating agreements that allowed two competing papers to merge business operations. But in the small and mid-sized markets, only one newspapers usually survived. These papers became de facto monopolies, the prime source of news in their communities as well as the only viable advertising option for local businesses. At many such newspapers, profit margins soared to 20 percent and even 40 percent. The large chains competed with one another to acquire these papers.

Some large companies—such as Hearst and the Newhouse/Advance group—chose to remain private and financed their acquisitions either through debt or profits from their own newspapers. Several big-name newspaper companies—Gannett, Knight Ridder, Lee, McClatchy, Pulitzer, Scripps, Dow Jones, The New York Times and The Washington Post—raised capital for acquisitions by selling stock on either the New York or American stock exchanges. Some bought television stations and magazines, too. By 2000, chains owned more than 90 percent of all American newspapers.[13] Most privately owned chains—for example, Shaw Media and Boone—were smaller than the publicly traded chains and typically confined themselves to a specific geographic region.

Publicly traded chains had to be attentive to their shareholders, a development that raised concerns as to whether powerful newspaper corporations would put shareholder expectation ahead of substantive journalism and their responsibilities to the community. However, since most newspapers sold for 13 times yearly earnings,[iv] large chains still had a strong financial incentive to take the long-term view when evaluating whether to purchase a newspaper.[14] To allay concerns, such publicly held companies as The New York Times, The Washington Post and Dow Jones created dual classes of stock, giving the founders' descendants controlling voting rights. Other chains, such as Knight Ridder, Times Mirror and McClatchy, focused on winning Pulitzer Prizes and other journalism awards to enhance their reputation, as well as their brand, in the marketplace.[15]

The transition to the current generation of newspaper baron began in the 1990s. The newspaper industry recorded historic levels of advertising revenue, profitability and circulation in the 1980s and 1990s.[16] Seeing that newspapers produced a steady and reliable source of income, institutional investors—including hedge and pension funds—bought shares in publicly traded newspaper companies.

At first, hedge and pension funds were, by and large, passive investors. In 2000, however, print advertising revenue began a dramatically steep decline. By 2005, some passive investors had become activist shareholders, pressing newspaper companies to pursue new strategies and advocating selling entire companies. In 2006, for example, three hedge funds, acting in concert, compelled Knight Ridder, with 61 papers and more than 4 million in circulation, to sell to McClatchy, then a much smaller company.[17]

The financial crisis and Great Recession of 2008–2009 exacerbated the already considerable economic woes of newspapers. With newspaper valuations at historic lows, hedge funds, private equity partnerships and publicly traded investment entities began snatching up hundreds of properties, mostly in small and mid-sized communities.

In 2004, the legacy chains of the 20th century still dominated the list of the nation's largest newspaper companies. By 2014, a mere decade later, they had been supplanted by the investment groups that had grown overnight by purchasing distressed legacy companies. The once-passive investors had become full-fledged owners and operators.

As if to distinguish themselves from the iconic newspaper chains of the previous century named after their founders, these new media barons adopted corporate-sounding names—New Media/GateHouse, Digital First, BH Media, Civitas, 10/13 Communications. Few in the top management ranks had journalistic experience or passion. They viewed newspapers as investments—one of many in their portfolio of businesses.

---

iv   Newspapers have historically been valued based on the financial benchmark EBITDA, which stands for "earnings before interest, taxes, depreciation and amortization" are deducted. The net income figure listed on a company's financial statements includes payments and deductions for these items, which can fluctuate widely year to year. Therefore EBITDA is considered a more reliable measure of a company's operating efficiency over the long term.

In the late 1990s, as newspaper profits soared, several privately held investment firms began to quietly purchase small newspaper chains as they came on the market. By 2004, two of these companies had accumulated more than 300 papers between them and had become the second- and fourth-largest chains in the country, in terms of number of newspapers owned. However, most of the papers they owned were in small markets, so their arrival went unnoticed by industry professionals and analysts, who focused on circulation in determining the biggest newspaper companies. Using circulation as a yardstick, the chains assembled in the latter half of the 20th century—Gannett, Knight Ridder and Advance, among others—still topped the list.

The size and span of influence of newspaper companies can be calculated either in terms of total circulation or number of papers owned. Until recently, the newspaper industry has largely used circulation as the primary standard.

And yet, in assessing the reach of newspaper owners across many communities, the number of papers controlled is an equally important measurement. In a city of 100,000, for example, a newspaper owner would have roughly the same influence whether its publication had circulation of 20,000 or 30,000. Meanwhile, an owner of four newspapers with 5,000 circulation in four towns would have influence in each of those localities, even with circulation below the newspaper in a mid-size city.

With circulation as a measurement, big-name, well-recognized companies founded in the 20th century dominated the field in 2004. Three of the largest five companies—Gannett, Knight Ridder and Tribune Co.—were publicly traded. They had combined circulation of 14.6 million. The third- and fifth-largest chains—Advance Publications and MediaNews Group—were private companies. They had a combined circulation of 6.8 million. The 10 largest companies had a combined circulation of 30 million, or more than a fourth of the total circulation in the country.

## THE LARGEST 10 COMPANIES BY CIRCULATION: 2004

Company Type: Public Investment Private

| Rank | Company | Total Papers | Daily Papers | Total Circ. (000s) | Daily Circ. (000s) |
|------|---------|--------------|--------------|--------------------|--------------------|
| 1 | Gannett | 177 | 95 | 6,796 | 5,044 |
| 2 | Knight Ridder | 4 | 37 | 4,184 | 3,849 |
| 3 | Advance Publications | 89 | 26 | 4,136 | 2,695 |
| 4 | Tribune Publishing | 34 | 13 | 3,620 | 3,262 |
| 5 | MediaNews Group | 97 | 46 | 2,697 | 2,099 |
| 6 | Journal Register Co. | 151 | 27 | 2,120 | 630 |
| 7 | Hearst Corporation | 20 | 12 | 1,852 | 1,579 |
| 8 | McClatchy | 27 | 12 | 1,604 | 1,397 |
| 9 | EW Scripps | 22 | 18 | 1,589 | 1,524 |
| 10 | Media General | 50 | 24 | 1,410 | 864 |

SOURCE: UNC Database

When the number of newspapers owned is used as a measurement, instead of circulation, a very different picture emerges. In 2004, the top five companies ranked by newspapers owned were Gannett, Liberty Group Publishing, the Journal Register Co., Community Newspaper Holdings and MediaNews Group.

Liberty Group Publishing and Community Newspaper Holdings Inc. (CNHI)—along with American Community Newspapers (ACN)—had been formed at the end of the 1990s, when newspaper revenue and profits were near their peak.[18]

For Knight Ridder, Advance and their legacy newspaper peers, ink-on-paper publications brought in robust revenue and profit, a portion of which financed their mission as providers of news and information.

In contrast, these three privately held investment entities—Liberty Group Publishing, CNHI and ACN—viewed newspapers as investments, pure and simple. Statements by these firms' investment managers described small newspapers, most with circulation of less than 10,000, as reliable and consistent sources of income for their portfolios of diverse business assets. Small rural markets, they believed, would be relatively insulated in the coming years from competition—either from traditional media, such as television, or the internet, which was then still in its infancy.

- Community Newspaper Holdings Inc. (CNHI) was founded in 1997, as part of a diverse portfolio of investments made by the Retirement Systems of Alabama. CNHI initially acquired papers from Media General and Hollinger International, as well as additional properties from Thomson in 2000 and Ottaway in 2002.[19]
- Liberty Group Publishing, established in 1998, was financed by Leonard Green & Partners LP, a Los Angeles-based private equity firm that specialized in turning around troubled companies. Liberty Group Publishing initially purchased 160 papers from Hollinger International, which was selling 40 percent of its U.S. community group in an effort to pay down debt.[20]
- American Community Newspapers was established in 1998 as Lionheart Holdings with the financial backing of Weiss, Peck & Greer's private equity group and Waller-Sutton Media Partners LP. It quickly grew through the acquisition of E.W. Scripps Co.'s Dallas Community Newspaper Group and three major purchases from families in Minnesota and Kansas. Lionheart Holdings was rebranded as American Community Newspapers in 2002.[21]

## LARGEST 25 COMPANIES IN 2004, RANKED BY NUMBER OF PAPERS OWNED

Company Type: Public Investment Private

| Rank | Company | Total Papers | Daily Papers | Total Circ. (000s) | Daily Circ. (000s) |
|------|---------|------------|------------|------------------|------------------|
| 1 | Gannett | 177 | 95 | 6,796 | 5,044 |
| 2 | Liberty Group Publishing | 159 | 65 | 838 | 347 |
| 3 | Journal Register Co. | 151 | 27 | 2,120 | 630 |
| 4 | CNHI | 149 | 86 | 1,256 | 890 |
| 5 | MediaNews Group | 97 | 46 | 2,698 | 2,099 |
| 6 | Herald Media | 92 | 3 | 828 | 297 |
| 7 | Advance Publications | 89 | 26 | 4,136 | 2,696 |
| 8 | Lee Enterprises | 79 | 43 | 1,377 | 1,109 |
| 9 | Ogden Newspapers | 71 | 38 | 937 | 569 |
| 10 | Knight Ridder | 64 | 37 | 4,185 | 3,849 |
| 11 | Landmark Media Enterprises | 61 | 8 | 960 | 466 |
| 12 | Pulitzer | 55 | 15 | 1,025 | 581 |
| 13 | Media General | 50 | 24 | 1,410 | 864 |
| 14 | Paxton Media Group | 50 | 28 | 532 | 333 |
| 15 | Freedom Communications | 45 | 22 | 1,301 | 857 |
| 16 | Hollinger International | 44 | 7 | 770 | 470 |
| 17 | American Community Newspapers | 44 | 2 | 417 | 12 |
| 18 | Morris Communications | 39 | 26 | 790 | 678 |
| 19 | Cox Newspapers | 38 | 17 | 1,260 | 1,092 |
| 20 | News Media Corporation | 38 | 5 | 165 | 24 |
| 21 | Morris Multimedia | 37 | 6 | 349 | 56 |
| 22 | Boone Newspapers | 37 | 12 | 294 | 67 |
| 23 | Rust Communications | 37 | 19 | 193 | 114 |
| 24 | Horizon Publications | 37 | 22 | 172 | 96 |
| 25 | Suffolk Life Newspapers | 36 | 0 | 533 | 0 |

SOURCE: UNC Database

See newspaperownership.com/additional-material/ for a list of newspapers owned by the largest 25 companies in 2004.

In 2004, these investment groups held 352 papers—or 20 percent of all the papers owned by the largest 25 companies. But because these companies had purchased small papers, they controlled only 7 percent of the circulation among the top 25 group.

All that would change over the coming turbulent decade as other investment groups moved in, displacing the media barons that dominated the charts in 2004. For their part, Liberty Group Publishing and American Community Newspapers went through multiple iterations over the course of the decade as the investment firm managers reshuffled their portfolio, making numerous acquisitions and divestitures. After bankruptcy in 2009, American Community Newspapers ceased to exist, its newspapers sold off to other large companies by its creditors.[22] After several financial restructurings, Liberty Group Publishing morphed into New Media Group/GateHouse. In 2014, only Community Newspaper Holdings Inc. existed much as it had in 2004, but with two dozen fewer newspapers.

Hedge funds and pension funds also began betting on newspapers in the 1990s, seeing them as "safe" investments. Numerous institutional investors began acquiring stock in publicly traded companies—such as Knight Ridder and The New York Times Co. As the migration of readers and advertisers to the internet increased in the early years of the 21st century, many began agitating boards and executives of these chains to make changes or sell their newspaper empires. In the wake of the 2008–2009 Great Recession, the valuations of newspapers dropped almost overnight. Suddenly passive investors—hedge funds and private equity funds—decided it was time to buy newspapers. Since 2010, they have been acquiring papers at bargain basement prices and assembling large chains.

Newspaper advertising revenue peaked in 2000 at $64 billion, adjusted for inflation. In the wake of the dot-com bust and the short recession that accompanied the 9/11 terrorist attacks, revenue declined sharply.

By 2004, various institutional investors—including hedge and pension funds—had accumulated between 40 and 57 percent of the shares in publicly traded media companies.[23] But each of the firms held only a small percentage of any company and were usually passive investors. The revenue plunge served as a wake-up call for hedge fund and pension fund managers, who began aggressively questioning newspaper executives about their digital strategies. Some lobbied boards of directors to "consider all strategic alternatives," including sale of the company.

In the years leading up to 2008, newspapers in small and mid-sized markets with very little competition typically sold for 13 times annual earnings. This meant that new purchasers needed to own a paper for at least 13 years in order to recoup their investment.[24] As entire legacy companies—such as Pulitzer and Knight Ridder—became available, other legacy companies became active bidders. In addition to paying a premium price to acquire a newspaper company, many buyers took on substantial debt.

In 2005, large public and private companies spent $3 billion acquiring papers from one another. Lee Enterprises led the way, paying $1.5 billion to acquire the Pulitzer group.[25]

In 2006, more than $10 billion changed hands, with the McClatchy Co., which had 27 papers in 2004, purchasing all of Knight Ridder's 61 papers for $4 billion. McClatchy then sold four papers to MediaNews Group and Hearst in a transaction valued at $1 billion.[26]

In 2007, sales hit $20 billion, driven by News Corp.'s $5.6 billion acquisition of Dow Jones and the $8.2 billion purchase of the Tribune Co. by Sam Zell, a real estate mogul and private equity fund manager.[27]

Between 2005 and 2008, newspaper advertising revenue continued its downward trajectory, even as newspaper publishers scrambled to sell more digital advertising to compensate for the loss of print revenue. Despite this, investors remained somewhat bullish on newspapers in small and mid-sized markets, where print advertising declined less rapidly.[28]

As the nation focused on a historic presidential election, and Wall Street and Main Street slipped toward a stunning downturn; 2008 turned out to be a pivotal year in newspaper ownership. The 2008–2009 Great Recession decimated the print advertising revenue of papers in both large and small markets. This paved the way for the transition of institutional investors from minority shareholders to outright owners and operators.

At the beginning of 2009, the market capitalization of publicly traded companies such as Gannett, McClatchy and Lee had fallen more than

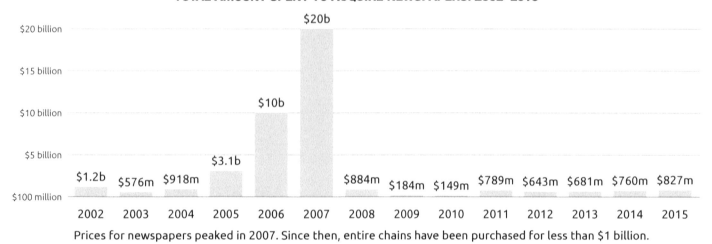

## TOTAL AMOUNT SPENT TO ACQUIRE NEWSPAPERS: 2002–2015

Prices for newspapers peaked in 2007. Since then, entire chains have been purchased for less than $1 billion.

SOURCE: Dirks, Van Essen & Murray

80 percent.[29] As a result, newspapers were being valued by investment firms that typically arranged financing at only three to five times yearly earnings. This meant acquirers could potentially sell, or "flip," a newspaper in three to five years and make a profit on the sale. Instead of the "buy and hold" strategy practiced by the legacy newspaper companies who had paid 13 times earnings before 2008, purchasers of newspapers since 2008 have been able "buy and sell" properties more frequently. Also, at substantially reduced sales prices, companies have been able to buy multiple newspapers for the same price they would have paid for only one previously.

The total amount of money spent on acquisitions spiked in 2007, fell dramatically in 2008 and has hovered below 2004 levels since.

Most of the major purchasers before 2008 took on substantial debt to pay for their acquisitions.[30] As newspapers' revenues and profits plummeted in the wake of the Great Recession, Lee Enterprises, Tribune Company and MediaNews Group, among others, were forced into bankruptcy proceedings by 2012.

With the large legacy companies mostly shut out of the market, recently formed investment companies were well-positioned to purchase not only newspapers at bargain prices, but also entire companies that had filed for bankruptcy or were disposing of properties to pay down debt. Consequently, by 2012, the number of major newspaper acquisitions had rebounded to previous levels. But, because of the lower valuations of newspapers, the total dollars spent on acquisitions has been less than $1 billion in every year since 2007. In 2010, the trough year, only $149 million was spent. By 2012 sales bounced back to $643 million and reached a post-recession high of $827 million in 2015.

More than a third of all newspapers — 2,906 — have changed ownership at least once since 2004. Newly formed investment firms — both privately held and publicly traded — have been the most aggressive purchasers since 2008. As a result, seven of the largest 25 newspaper companies by 2014 were investment firms.

The path from 2004 to today has been a convoluted one, featuring high newspaper turnover, numerous company mergers and acquisitions, and new actors entering the fray. Ten of the 25 largest companies in 2004 were purchased either in full or in part by other companies. Six of the largest 25 companies in 2014 had not existed in their current form in 2004, including five investment firms. Six privately owned traditional newspaper companies grew enough to make the list, three other private companies dropped off the list and one (Suffolk Life Newspapers) ceased operations.

By 2014, six of the 10 largest newspaper owners, measured by their number of newspapers, were investment entities:

- Liberty Group Publishing, purchased by Fortress Investment Group in 2005, morphed into New Media/GateHouse and became the largest chain, with 379 newspapers.[31]
- Digital First Media, formed in 2011, was the second largest, with 208 papers.
- Community Newspaper Holdings Inc., formed in 1997, had 21 fewer papers than in 2004, but still ranked fourth with 128 papers.
- Sixth-ranked Civitas Media, formed in 2012, had 98 papers.
- Tribune Publishing was seventh largest, with 95 papers; it had gone through two corporate restructurings and a bankruptcy between 2008 and 2014.
- BH Media, a division of Berkshire Hathaway formed in 2012, had 76 newspapers and was the ninth-largest company.[32]

In all, seven investment entities ranked among the largest 25 newspaper owners in the country in 2014, including the 18th largest, 10/13 Communications, formed in 2009.

## LARGEST 25 COMPANIES IN 2014, RANKED BY NUMBER OF PAPERS OWNED

Company Type: Public Investment Private

| Rank | Company | Total Papers | Daily Papers | Total Circ. (000s) | Daily Circ. (000s) |
|---|---|---|---|---|---|
| 1 | New Media/ GateHouse | 379 | 119 | 3,138 | 1,725 |
| 2 | Digital First Media | 208 | 79 | 4,574 | 3,067 |
| 3 | Gannett | 197 | 82 | 4,884 | 3,015 |
| 4 | CNHI | 128 | 77 | 1,159 | 825 |
| 5 | Lee Enterprises | 111 | 52 | 1,520 | 1,212 |
| 6 | Civitas Media | 98 | 35 | 694 | 312 |
| 7 | Tribune Publishing | 95 | 18 | 3,444 | 2,137 |
| 8 | Shaw Media | 82 | 9 | 450 | 115 |
| 9 | BH Media | 76 | 31 | 1,367 | 1,088 |
| 10 | Ogden Newspapers | 75 | 31 | 1,367 | 1,088 |
| 11 | Advance Publications | 74 | 21 | 2,714 | 1,396 |
| 12 | McClatchy | 69 | 29 | 2,921 | 1,943 |
| 13 | Landmark Media Enterprises | 57 | 4 | 550 | 182 |
| 14 | Boone Newspapers | 53 | 22 | 355 | 154 |
| 15 | Paxton Media Group | 51 | 30 | 406 | 281 |
| 16 | Community Media Group | 51 | 10 | 228 | 57 |
| 17 | News Media Corporation | 48 | 3 | 195 | 17 |
| 18 | 10/13 Communications | 47 | 3 | 948 | 49 |
| 19 | North Jersey Media Group | 46 | 2 | 662 | 186 |
| 20 | Black Press Group | 45 | 9 | 1,118 | 426 |
| 21 | Stephens Media | 44 | 9 | 1,100 | 315 |
| 22 | Rust Communications | 44 | 18 | 185 | 104 |
| 23 | ECM Publishers | 42 | 1 | 472 | 3 |
| 24 | Forum Communications | 41 | 11 | 409 | 183 |
| 25 | Adams Publishing Group | 38 | 9 | 305 | 83 |

SOURCE: UNC Database

See newspaperownership.com/additional-material/ for a list of newspapers owned by the largest 25 companies in 2014.

The seven investment entities owned twice as many dailies in 2014 as in 2004, and three times as many nondailies. They controlled six times as much circulation, expanding from 2.5 million in 2004 to 15.3 million in 2014. Consequently, ranked in size by circulation, four of the largest 10 newspaper companies in 2014 were also investment entities.

- Digital First Media was second largest, with 4.5 million circulation
- Tribune Publishing was third, with 3.4 million.
- New Media/GateHouse, fourth largest, had 3.1 million
- BH Media, ninth, had 1.4 million

## THE LARGEST 10 COMPANIES BY CIRCULATION: 2014

Company Type: Public Investment Private

| Rank | Company | Total Papers | Daily Papers | Total Circ. (000s) | Daily Circ. (000s) |
|---|---|---|---|---|---|
| 1 | Gannett | 197 | 82 | 4,884 | 3,015 |
| 2 | Digital First Media | 208 | 79 | 4,574 | 3,067 |
| 3 | Tribune Publishing | 95 | 18 | 3,444 | 2,137 |
| 4 | New Media/ GateHouse | 379 | 119 | 3,138 | 1,725 |
| 5 | McClatchy | 69 | 29 | 2,923 | 1,943 |
| 6 | Advance Publications | 74 | 21 | 2,714 | 1,396 |
| 7 | Lee Enterprises | 111 | 52 | 1,520 | 1,213 |
| 8 | Hearst Corporation | 29 | 15 | 1,386 | 958 |
| 9 | BH Media | 76 | 31 | 1,367 | 1,088 |
| 10 | Nash Holdings (Jeff Bezos) | 32 | 2 | 1,334 | 665 |

SOURCE: UNC Database

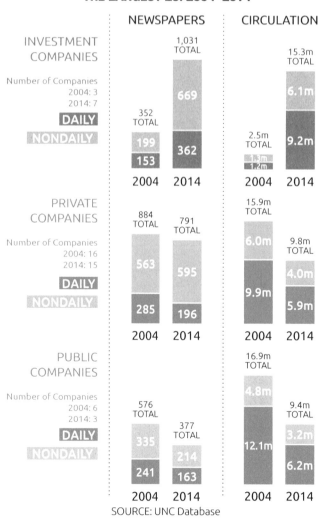

## HOW OWNERSHIP CHANGED AMONG THE LARGEST 25: 2004–2014

SOURCE: UNC Database

As investor ownership expanded, the number of large publicly traded companies declined from six to only three. By 2014, Knight Ridder, Pulitzer and Media General had been acquired by one of the other large companies. This left only Gannett, Lee and McClatchy among the 25 largest companies.

Gannett remained the largest company as ranked by total circulation, and the third largest in terms of newspapers owned. Lee had become the fifth largest in terms of number of newspapers, and eighth largest in circulation. McClatchy was the fifth largest in circulation and 12th largest in numbers of papers.

Overall, the number of newspapers owned by the largest publicly traded companies had dropped to 377, from 576, and the combined circulation had declined to 9.3 million, from 16.9 million.

There was also turnover among the largest private chains. Some, such as Advance and Hearst, hunkered down and remained largely intact. Others, such as MediaNews and Suffolk, filed for bankruptcy and were purchased by investment firms or closed.[33] Still, others—especially the small regional chains such as Boone and Rust—selectively acquired papers that came on the market in the post-recession years. As a result, the overall number of newspapers owned by the 16 largest private companies fell only slightly, to 791 in 2014, from 848 in 2004. However, combined circulation for the large private companies declined by a third—to 9.8 million.

By 2014, the seven largest investment groups dominated both in terms of number of newspapers owned and total circulation. They owned 240 newspapers more than the 16 largest private chains and 654 more than the three publicly traded chains. Their combined circulation had grown from a paltry 2.5 million in 2004 to 15.3 million, surpassing the total circulations of both the large private and public chains.

At the end of 2014, the seven largest investment groups owned 362 dailies and 669 nondailies. Almost 90 percent of their 1,031 newspapers were acquired after 2004, their largest transactions occurring between 2010 and 2012.

Investment companies have aggressively sought to expand their newspaper portfolios over the past decade.

Digital First, Civitas, BH Media and 10/13 Communications were all founded during the 2009–2012 period. New Media/GateHouse and Tribune emerged from bankruptcy in 2012 and 2013 and joined the pack in pursuit of more papers. Here's a graphic presentation of how the companies grew, based on press releases and news accounts.

(For year-by-year details on acquisitions and divestures of the largest investment companies, see newspaperownership.com/additional-material/.)

## NEWSPAPERS ACQUIRED, SOLD, MERGED, OR CLOSED: 2004–2016

**ACQUIRED  SOLD  CLOSED/MERGED**

| Company | Category | 2004 | 2005 | 2006 | 2007 | 2008 | 2009 | 2010 | 2011 | 2012 | 2013 | 2014 | 2015 | 2016 |
|---|---|---|---|---|---|---|---|---|---|---|---|---|---|---|
| New Media/GateHouse | Acquired | 2 | 266 | 140 | 45 | 2 | | | | | 23 | 54 | 73 | 27 |
| | Sold | 7 | | | 2 | 11 | | | | 35 | 8 | | 6 | 10 |
| | Closed/Merged | | | | | | 19 | | | | 13 | | 6 | 2 |
| Digital First | Acquired | | | 4 | 1 | | | | 144 | | | | | 28 |
| | Sold | | | | 13 | | | | | | | | 10 | 5 |
| | Closed/Merged | | | | | | | | | | | 8 | 7 | 6 |
| CNHI | Acquired | | 10 | 9 | | | | | | | | | | |
| | Sold | 23 | 1 | 5 | 5 | 1 | | | | 1 | 2 | 2 | 2 | |
| | Closed/Merged | | | | | | | | | | 1 | 3 | | |
| Civitas | Acquired | | | | | | | | 44 | 59 | | | | |
| | Sold | | | | | | | | | | | | 3 | |
| | Closed/Merged | | | | | | | | | | 8 | 2 | 2 | |
| tronc/Tribune | Acquired | | | 1 | | | | | | | | 56 | 9 | |
| | Sold | | | | 3 | 2 | | | | | | | | |
| | Closed/Merged | | | | 1 | | | | | | | | | |
| BH Media | Acquired | | | | | | | | 1 | 65 | 4 | | 7 | |
| | Sold | | | | | | | | | | | | | |
| | Closed/Merged | | | | | | | | | 1 | | 2 | | |
| 10/13 Communications | Acquired | | | | 1 | | | 3 | 15 | 28 | 2 | 1 | | |
| | Sold | | | | | | | | | | | | | 2 |
| | Closed/Merged | | | | | | | | | | | | | |

SOURCE: UNC Database & Various Press Releases

Number of newspapers listed may not reflect total shown in press releases, which may include non-community newspapers (i.e. shoppers, business journals, etc.).

Large newspaper-owning investment entities have financial and corporate profiles distinctly different from the newspaper chains that preceded them. These investment firms are relatively new to owning newspapers and managing them. The newspapers they own are often part of a portfolio of non-newspaper properties, including real estate, retail establishments and financial services.

Perhaps the biggest difference between the new newspaper barons and their predecessors is their pivot *away from* a long-term commitment to local journalism and the communities their newspapers have historically served *toward* a short-term investment and management strategy. In annual letters to shareholders, public statements by executives and press releases on their websites, the investment owners clearly acknowledge their laserlike focus on financial return.

For example, Warren Buffett's 2012 annual letter to shareholders explained that Berkshire Hathaway buys newspapers as attractive investments, given their low purchase cost and their de facto monopoly status in small and mid-sized markets.[34] Buffett has also made clear his willingness to shed his firm's stake in newspapers and move onto other investments as conditions change. In his 2014 shareholder letter, he described Berkshire Hathaway's readiness to redeploy capital from a declining operation: "At Berkshire, we can—without incurring taxes or much in the way of other costs—move huge sums from businesses that have limited opportunities for incremental investment to other sectors with greater promise. Moreover, we are free of historical biases created by lifelong association with a given industry and are not subject to pressures from colleagues having a vested interest in maintaining the status quo. That's important: If horses had controlled investment decisions, there would have been no auto industry."[35]

As a group, large investment firms that own newspapers share at least five of the following eight characteristics:

- **The stated emphasis of the parent company is to maximize shareholder return on investment.** They do not state an equal commitment to journalism and the community. (See http://newspaperownership.com/additional-information/ for a sampling of statements made by managers and executives of investment companies.)
- **Many properties were acquired as a group from other media companies through either purchase of entire companies or divisions.** Nine of the largest newspaper owners in 2004 were purchased in full or in part by investment firms.
- **Majority financial and/or operational control of the firm is held by a small number of institutional shareholders, such as lenders, private equity firms or investment fund managers.** Three are fully owned by private equity partnerships and one by a pension fund. In the three publicly traded companies, lenders or other types of institutional investors hold enough shares to determine the fate of the company.
- **The company was formed or incorporated within the past two decades and is a relative newcomer to newspaper ownership.** Five of the seven investment entities were formed in the past decade.

# DEFINING CHARACTERISTICS OF AN INVESTMENT COMPANY

| CHARACTERISTICS | NewMedia/ GateHouse | Digital First | CNHI | Civitas | tronc/ Tribune | BH Media | 10/13 Communications |
|---|---|---|---|---|---|---|---|
| The stated emphasis of the parent company is to maximize shareholder return on investment | X | X | X | X | X | X | X |
| Many properties were acquired as a group from other media companies through either purchase of entire companies or divisions. | X | X | X | X | X | X | X |
| Majority financial and/or operational control of the firm is held by a small number of institutional shareholders, such as lenders, private equity firms or investment fund managers. | X | X | X | X | | X | |
| The company was formed or incorporated within the past two decades and is a relative newcomer to newspaper ownership. | X | X | X | X | | X | X |
| The newspaper holdings are part of a portfolio of non-newspaper companies. | X | X | X | X | | X | X |
| There has been much movement of individual newspapers within portfolios. | X | X | X | X | X | | |
| There have been two or more financial restructurings, including bankruptcy reorganization, a rebranding after selling the company or flips between public and private ownership. | X | X | | X | X | | |
| A private equity company, a hedge fund or penion fund has at some point during the past decade owned all or a significant portion of the enterprise. | X | X | X | X | X | | X |

See http://newspaperownership.com/additional-material/ for details on the characteristics of each of the seven largest investment groups.

- **The newspaper holdings are part of a portfolio of non-newspaper companies.** The diverse business interests of these new newspaper owners include auto dealerships, real estate, financial instruments, distressed retailers, manufacturing firms and pharmaceutical and transportation companies, to name a few.
- **There has been much movement of individual newspapers within portfolios.** More than a third of all newspapers changed ownership in the past decade, many of which have been bought and sold two or more times.

- **There have been two or more financial restructurings, including bankruptcy reorganization, a rebranding after selling the company or flips between public and private ownership.** Four of the companies have filed for bankruptcy; two have flipped from either public to private or private to public.
- **A private equity company, a hedge fund or pension fund has at some point during the past decade owned all or a significant portion of the enterprise.** Four are owned either by a private equity fund, hedge fund or a pension fund. Two of the three publicly traded companies have been owned for at least a year by private equity funds.

The American press exercises a freedom guaranteed in the Constitution. Newspapers have almost always been run as for-profit businesses, but with a special civic role in the nation and in their local communities. In turn, the public has an interest in the companies and people who exercise the freedom and power of the news media. It is very difficult to ascertain the intentions of the new newspaper owners. The websites of the newspapers they own invariably proclaim their commitment to public service journalism. Yet the press releases and publicly available material of the investment partnerships that own these newspapers focus on financial return for shareholders.

While UNC researchers were assembling the data in this report on new media barons, The New York Times was independently reporting on the movement by private equity entities into delivering local and state government services.[36] The Times report on Fortress Investment Group did not mention that the firm now owns more newspapers—under the New Media/GateHouse brand—than any other chain, but it provided this insight into the sweep of the holdings of major investment entities:

*"While little known outside Wall Street, Fortress covers a cross section of American life through companies it owns or manages. It controls the nation's largest nonbank collector of mortgage payments. It is building one of the country's few private passenger railroads. It helps oversee a company that manages public golf courses in several states."*

In this context, the rise of new media barons raises questions of accountability and transparency: Who makes decisions on overall strategic direction and content of the newspapers these firms manage? What's the structure of these newspaper-owning companies?

Publicly traded newspaper companies are required to submit quarterly and annual reports with audited financial statements and management assessments of the business.[37] Still, financial statements of the three publicly traded investment companies—New Media/GateHouse, BH Media and Tribune—are difficult to decipher, especially as they relate to the performance of their newspaper properties and their long-term strategy for them.

Private investment companies are required to disclose only the most basic information.[38]

Here is a summary of relevant financial developments of major newspaper-owning investment firms from what can be ascertained from publicly available information, including company websites and press releases:

### New Media/GateHouse (Fortress Investment Group): 379 Newspapers in 2014

In 2005, the private equity firm Fortress Investment Group (FIG) entered the newspaper business by purchasing the Liberty Publishing Group from Leonard Green & Partners, a Los Angeles-based investor. Fortress has $70.5 billion in assets under management and describes itself on the company website as "a leading, highly diversified global investment management firm" that "applies its deep experience and specialized expertise across a range of investment strategies—private equity, credit, liquid markets and traditional asset management—on behalf of over 1,600 institutional investors and private clients worldwide." In 2006, Fortress took the Liberty Group Publishing public under the GateHouse brand. A year later, Fortress, itself, became the first large private equity company to list its shares on the New York Stock Exchange.

In 2013, after purchasing the Dow Jones Local Media Group through Newcastle Investment, a company owned and managed by Fortress,[39] GateHouse filed for reorganization through a pre-packaged bankruptcy. All newspaper properties were transferred into a newly created subsidiary called New Media Investment Group, also publicly traded.[40,41] Fortress assumed the majority of the debt and management of New Media, and in return receives stock, stock options and a management fee of 1.5 percent based on the value of the stock. Some of the largest shareholders in New Media include Vanguard, T. Rowe Price and BlackRock.[42] Since emerging from bankruptcy, Fortress, under the New Media/GateHouse brand, has continued to expand and has pledged to fund $1 billion in acquisitions through 2016.[43] Today, New Media has a market capitalization of about $640 million, accounting for less than 1 percent of Fortress' $70.5 billion in assets.

### Digital First Media: 208 Newspapers in 2014
Alden Global Capital, a privately owned hedge fund operator, founded Digital First Media in 2011 as a subsidiary that included newspapers in the MediaNews Group and Journal Register Co. Alden had assumed ownership of the MediaNews Group in 2010 and Journal Register in 2011 through bankruptcy proceedings. The Journal Register, which was the third-largest newspaper company in 2004 with 151 papers, had sold off more than half of its papers by the time Alden Capital assumed ownership. MediaNews and Journal Register were formally merged in 2013. Alden has also purchased outstanding debt from a number of private newspaper owners, including Freedom Communications. Digital First acquired The Orange County Register, owned by Freedom Communications, in bankruptcy proceedings in 2016.

Because Alden is privately held, there is little available information on the finances of the company or its owner/founder, Randall Smith.[44] In 2014, Alden announced its intention to sell Digital First Media. Two private equity groups — Cerberus Capital Management and Apollo Global Management — expressed interest in purchasing the company, but the deal for the entire company never materialized.[45] Since then, Digital First Media has acquired Freedom Communications, while also quietly disposing of some properties. Recently, it has sold The Salt Lake (Utah) Tribune to Paul Huntsman, brother of former Gov. Jon Huntsman Jr., as well as its small papers in southern Vermont and northwestern Massachusetts to a group of local businessmen.

### Community Newspaper Holdings (CNHI): 128 Newspapers in 2014
CNHI was created in 1997 as a holding company for the Retirement Systems of Alabama to purchase newspapers. The Alabama retirement enterprise manages 23 investment funds. The income from CNHI makes up such a small portion of the diversified $36.6 billion investment portfolio that it is not broken out in annual reports. Since 2004, the company has made only small acquisitions, usually purchasing independently owned and operated papers in small markets. During the same period, it has sold or closed more than three dozen of its underperforming newspapers.

### Civitas Media: 98 Newspapers in 2014
Versa Capital Management, a private equity firm based in Philadelphia, formed Civitas Media in 2012[46] when it combined four media subsidiaries the company had bought in bankruptcy or financial distress. Those four were Freedom Central, a division of Freedom Communications; Heartland Publications; Impressions Media, and Ohio Community Media (Brown Publishing). Since forming Civitas Media, the firm has not made any major acquisitions. As of 2015, Versa had $1.4 billion[47] in assets under management, including ownership of retailers, restaurants and manufacturers. According to its website, Versa Capital focuses on buying "distressed properties."[48] The company's target criteria for acquisitions include "Chapter 11 or Out-of-Court Restructurings" and "Reorganizations & Liquidations."[49]

### tronc/Tribune Publishing: 95 Newspapers in 2014
In 2007, the publicly traded media company, which included radio and television stations, as well the Los Angeles Times and Chicago Tribune, was purchased for $8.2 billion by investor Sam Zell, who then took the company private, financed primarily with debt.[50] Zell is founder and chairman of a private investment firm, Equity Group Investments, which has a diverse portfolio of assets, including real estate, energy, transportation and retail. The Tribune Co. filed for Chapter 11 bankruptcy in 2008, listing $7.6 billion in assets against a debt of $13 billion.[51]

In 2012, the company emerged from bankruptcy under the control of its institutional creditors, including JPMorgan Chase & Co., Oaktree Capital Management LP and Angelo, Gordon & Co. In 2014, the Tribune newspapers were spun off from the broadcasting assets with $350 million in debt, and the restructured company began trading again on the New York Stock Exchange as Tribune Publishing. The publishing company made its first acquisition in 2014, buying the suburban newspaper group of the Chicago Sun-Times. In 2016, Michael Ferro, owner of the Chicago Sun-Times, began accumulating shares of Tribune Publishing through his private equity firm, Merrick Ventures LLC, after donating his shares of the Chicago Sun-Times to an unnamed charitable trust to alleviate concerns about a conflict of interest.[52] Since becoming CEO and publisher, Ferro has brought in health tech investor Nant Capital, managed by Patrick Soon-Shiong, part-owner of the Los Angeles Lakers. The two investment firms owned 27 percent of the stock of tronc at the end of June 2016 and have the ability to purchase up to 50 percent of the shares.[53]

### BH Media: 76 Newspapers in 2014
Berkshire Hathaway, the international conglomerate and holding company founded by Warren Buffett, has a market capitalization of $368 billion.[54] It owns a diverse portfolio, including insurance, clothing, manufacturing and retail. BH Media was formed as a newspaper subsidiary in 2011 after Berkshire Hathaway purchased the Omaha World-Herald in Buffett's Nebraska hometown. In 2012, BH Media bought Media General's newspapers.[55] Since then, BH Media has expanded through acquisitions of smaller newspapers. Revenues from BH Media account for less than 1 percent of total Berkshire Hathaway revenues.[56]

In contrast to investment fund managers who are relative newcomers to the newspaper industry, Buffett's experience dates back to the mid-1970s ,when he purchased The Buffalo News and was appointed to the board of directors of The Washington Post Co., a position he held for more than two decades.

In his 2012 annual shareholder letter, Buffett devoted an entire section to explaining his rationale in purchasing Media General. With earnings multiples, which determine purchase price, at historic lows, local newspapers, he said, were especially attractive acquisitions, and with a "sensible" digital strategy, they should be viable for years to come. But he also said that BH Media was willing to shutter any newspaper operating at a loss, citing the closing in 2012 of the Manassas News & Messenger, a 10,000-circulation daily in Virginia. In 2016, Buffett stressed that all his papers are profitable, "but the trend lines are discouraging." With the exception of national papers, he said, "no one has cracked the code" to developing a sustainable business model.[57]

### 10/13 Communications: 47 Newspapers in 2014
This private investment firm, formed in 2009, is a partnership between 10K Investments, owned by two Reno, Nevada, businessmen, and 13th Street Media, owned by Randy Miller, who previously owned the Boulder (CO) Daily Camera before selling it to E.W. Scripps in 2005. 10K investor Arne Hoel has served on the boards of Swift Communications, which owns small newspapers in Colorado and California, and American Consolidated Media, which sold its 100 newspapers to Adams Publishing Group and New Media/GateHouse. Hoel's partner, Brett Coleman, sold a residential construction company in 2005 and has no previous newspaper experience. Since its formation, 10/13 Communications has made three major acquisitions: Freedom Communications' Phoenix assets, the Dallas operations of American Community Newspapers and ASP Westward's Houston newspapers. The company also bought the ITZ Group, a digital consulting company, in 2013.

Since 2014, the big chains have grown even bigger. Some legacy companies have re-entered the market and begun bidding against the investment groups. Most notably, in 2016, Gannett made two major purchases—Scripps/Journal Media and North Jersey Media. Meanwhile, New Media/GateHouse, Digital First and BH Media have continued to acquire newspapers and newspaper chains. The acquisition sprees of the largest companies have begun to raise questions. Among them: How big is too big? Are the measurements used to determine "monopoly" in a local market still valid in a digital era? What are the responsibilities of the owners of these large chains of newspapers to the communities where these papers are located?

As of mid-2016, the three largest newspaper chains—New Media, Gannett and Digital First—own 898 newspapers, nearly twice as many as the three largest chains in 2004. They control a combined 12.7 million in circulation.

- New Media/GateHouse owns 432 papers in 32 states and controls 3.6 million in circulation.
- Gannett currently owns 258 papers in 34 states and has 5.2 million in circulation. In recent months, Gannett has made two unsolicited attempts to buy tronc/Tribune. If brought to fruition, such an acquisition would add 104 newspapers with 3.4 million in circulation to Gannett's portfolio.
- Digital First owns 208 papers in 15 states and has 3.9 million in circulation.

Here are the major purchases made by the three largest companies:

- New Media/GateHouse purchased 39 local papers in 2015 for $102.5 million from the privately held company, Stephens Media.[58]
- Gannett, after spinning off its broadcast properties in 2015 into a separate company called Tegna, emerged debt-free and immediately began buying newspapers again.[59] It has purchased 20 papers from the Journal Media group[60] and 11 papers in Texas that had been jointly owned with Digital First.[61] Most recently it purchased 46 newspapers from the North Jersey Media Group.[62]
- Digital First added 22 papers that had previously been part of Freedom Communications,[63] but also shed 18, including the Salt Lake Tribune[64] and several smaller papers in New England. In addition, it merged several papers.[65]

Tribune Publishing, renamed tronc in 2016, is now the sixth-largest chain, in terms of number of papers, up from seventh place in 2014. It bought the San Diego Union-Tribune and its accompanying community newspapers for $85 million.[66] It also rejected two bids by Gannett to purchase the company at 5.5 times annual earnings.[67]

Two privately held newspapers companies—Adams Publishing Group and Boone Newspapers—were also active purchasers of small-market papers in 2015. Adams Publishing Group, a family investment fund formed in 2014 to buy and operate small newspaper chains in Ohio, purchased 24 community papers from Nash Holdings, which also owns The Washington Post.[68] Adams now holds 52 papers. Boone Newspapers, which prefers to buy family-owned papers or small chains, purchased nine more papers and now owns 61 papers.

If Gannett succeeds in acquiring tronc/Tribune, it will own 362 papers in 36 states and control 8.6 million in circulation—more than six times the circulation of the Wall Street Journal and more than twice the circulation of all the 432 papers owned by New Media/GateHouse.

The largest newspaper companies are larger than ever before. Until recently, however, the government had expressed little concern about the merger and acquisition activity. Then, early in 2016, the Department of Justice sued to stop Tribune Publishing from purchasing Freedom Communications, citing antitrust concerns. Tribune would have a dominant market share in southern California if it owned the two Freedom papers—the Orange County Register and Riverside Press-Enterprise—as well as the San Diego Union-Tribune and the Los Angeles Times.[69] Digital First Media, which had submitted a lower bid than Tribune, then purchased Freedom Communications for $52.3 million from local owner Aaron Kushner, who had filed for bankruptcy.

Consolidation usually occurs in a mature industry dealing with declining revenues and profit margins. The remaining firms attempt to achieve economies of scale with both costs and revenues. The large chains—including many of the legacy newspaper owners—assume that they need to own many papers in many regions to attract advertising and to hold down costs. This raises the question: Is consolidation the only answer, and will it pay the bills much longer if the industry does not develop new business models?

It is difficult to predict if the fevered pace of the past decade will continue. Or if the new media barons—the large investment entities—will continue to be the dominant buyers and operators. They may choose to divest their newspaper holdings and move on to other more attractive options.

The massive consolidation and reshuffling of ownership since 2004 has both short-term and long-term ramifications for communities that have historically depended on their newspapers to provide them with the news and information that strengthens democracy and capitalism at the local level. The larger the chains become, the more detached and disconnected newspaper owners become from the communities their newspapers have historically served. The next section, "The Emerging Threat of News Deserts," considers what is at stake for both the industry and communities across the country.

## LARGEST 25 COMPANIES RANKED BY NUMBER OF PAPERS OWNED: 2016

Company Type: Public Investment Private

| Rank | Company | Total Papers | Daily Papers | Total Circ. (000s) | Daily Circ. (000s) |
|------|---------|--------------|--------------|--------------------|--------------------|
| 1 | New Media/GateHouse | 432 | 125 | 3,577 | 1,813 |
| 2 | Gannett | 258 | 109 | 5,171 | 3,292 |
| 3 | Digital First Media | 208 | 62 | 2,941 | 2,038 |
| 4 | CNHI | 125 | 75 | 1,105 | 727 |
| 5 | Lee Enterprises | 113 | 52 | 1,335 | 867 |
| 6 | tronc/Tribune | 104 | 19 | 3,433 | 2,054 |
| 7 | Civitas Media | 90 | 34 | 693 | 332 |
| 8 | Shaw Media | 83 | 9 | 439 | 87 |
| 9 | Ogden Newspapers | 82 | 41 | 747 | 434 |
| 10 | BH Media | 80 | 33 | 1,321 | 947 |
| 11 | Advance Publications | 74 | 21 | 2,491 | 1,142 |
| 12 | McClatchy | 68 | 29 | 2,538 | 1,516 |
| 13 | Boone Newspapers | 61 | 26 | 367 | 174 |
| 14 | Landmark Media Enterprises | 57 | 4 | 552 | 156 |
| 15 | Paxton Media Group | 53 | 32 | 473 | 328 |
| 16 | Adams Publishing Group | 52 | 14 | 438 | 133 |
| 17 | Community Media Group | 52 | 11 | 289 | 63 |
| 18 | News Media Corporation | 48 | 3 | 219 | 17 |
| 19 | Black Press Group | 47 | 9 | 1,375 | 507 |
| 20 | 10/13 Communications | 45 | 3 | 860 | 60 |
| 21 | Rust Communications | 44 | 18 | 236 | 135 |
| 22 | ECM Publishers | 42 | 1 | 486 | 2 |
| 23 | Forum Communications | 41 | 11 | 355 | 154 |
| 24 | Horizon Publications | 32 | 22 | 142 | 91 |
| 25 | Trib Publications | 35 | 0 | 118 | 0 |

SOURCE: UNC Database

See newspaperownership.com/additional-material/ for a list of newspapers owned by the largest 25 companies in 2016.

# THE EMERGING THREAT
# OF NEWS DESERTS

Today, Americans have access to more news than ever, available round-the-clock, delivered through the internet to smartphones and laptops and by cable and satellite to TV sets. Out of the digital deluge of news come up-close-and-personal videos of terrorist attacks, of violence by and to police officers, of full-length speeches by presidential candidates, as well as features on celebrities and how-to advice on every subject imaginable. And yet the digital deluge hardly spills out *local* news.

In states and some larger cities, niche online news organizations have sprung up to fill gaps left by the downsizing of metropolitan newspapers. But for residents in smaller cities and towns, from Goldsboro, North Carolina, to Minot, North Dakota, the internet offers little substantive coverage of events and issues of everyday interest and importance. Unless local newspapers in those communities reconstruct themselves and sustain their coverage online, who will pay attention to the actions of the city council, the success of local schools, or the safety of the town's water supply?

In the 20th century, newspaper publishers used revenue from selling print advertising to pay for public service journalism, the day-to-day reporting and commentary that inform citizens and improve the quality of life in a community. That old model no longer delivers sufficient revenue, and newspaper owners are struggling to come up with a new one. Legacy owners, such as McClatchy and Advance, as well as newcomers, such as New Media/Gatehouse and BH Media, have made painful cuts in expenses. Overall newsroom staffing has fallen below 1970s levels. Even among the surviving newspapers, the editorial scope and influence of newspapers have diminished.

Some new media barons — New Media/GateHouse, Digital First, tronc and 10/13 Communications — have also implemented aggressive digital strategies, aimed at capturing new readers and at opening a wider revenue stream. But in chasing "clicks" and "audiences" to appeal to local advertisers, their cookie-cutter newspaper websites and social media postings supply pithy and entertaining features for "sharing," "listicles" and the sort of videos ubiquitous on the internet.[70]

Ultimately, it doesn't matter whether local news is delivered through ink-on-paper or over a mobile phone. What matters is that a local news organization reports on important issues and provides context and analysis so citizens can make informed decisions and hold their public officials accountable.

Unprecedented consolidation in the newspaper industry has placed the fate of local journalism into the hands of fewer companies than ever before. The largest chains have grown so large that they necessarily have less attachment to the communities where they own newspapers than even the barons of previous eras. The rise of the newest media owners, with their emphasis on profit benchmarks instead of civic responsibility, has added a new wrinkle.

In the late 19th and early 20th century, many newspapers adopted slogans that touted their public service mission: "All the News That's Fit to Print" or "The Only Newspaper in the World That Gives a Damn About Yerington (Nevada)." The now-defunct Cleveland Press, which *Time* magazine identified in 1964 as one of the top 10 local newspapers in America, had a straightforward motto: "The Newspaper That Serves Its Readers." By contrast, a manager's manual from the investment firm 10/13 Communications, established in 2009 espouses a different sentiment: "Our customer is the advertiser. Readers are our customers' customers. [Therefore] we operate with a lean newsroom staff."[71]

Over the past decade, investment firms have acquired significantly more newspapers in rural areas or localities with high poverty rates. With regional news outlets — including metro papers and television stations — pulling back coverage from outlying areas, newspapers owned by investment entities are often the only source of local news in many communities. Because they spread risk across multiple products and geographic areas, investment groups can afford to let individual newspapers fail or pursue a harvesting strategy in which they "manage the decline" of the assets in their portfolio. If their newspapers fail, and viable alternatives do not arise, many communities across the country are in danger of becoming news deserts.

THE NATIONAL FOOTPRINT OF THE LARGEST 25 CHAINS

In 2016, the largest 25 companies—seven investment entities, three public companies and 15 private firms—collectively own newspapers in all 50 states. In all but a handful of states, they own the largest two or three dailies, as well as dozens of smaller dailies and weeklies.

The large chain-owned papers are concentrated in the eastern half of the U.S. and along the Pacific Coast. Ten less-densely populated states in the Rocky Mountain and Western Great Plains region have fewer newspapers, most owned by smaller, regional private companies.

The two largest companies have the biggest national footprint. New Media/GateHouse currently owns 432 local newspapers in 32 states, while Gannett has 258 papers in 34 states. The other large companies have much smaller footprints. Their newspapers tend to cluster in specific geographic regions of the country. Digital First, the third-largest company, owns 208 papers in only 15 states. Similarly, Advance, one of the largest privately owned chains, has 74 papers in 11 states.

### WHERE NEWSPAPERS OWNED BY THE 25 LARGEST CHAINS ARE LOCATED: 2016

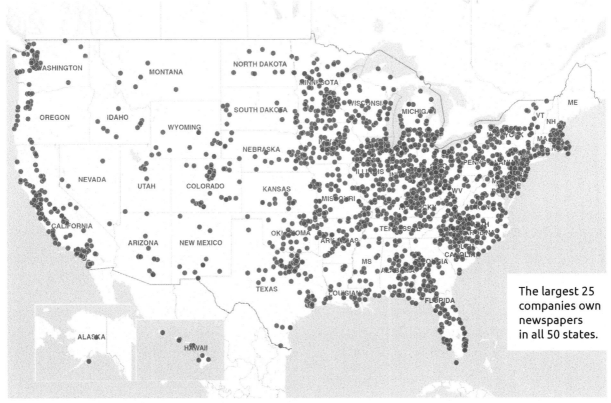

The largest 25 companies own newspapers in all 50 states.

SOURCE: UNC Database

See newspaperownership.com/map/ to see if one of the 25 largest companies owns the newspaper in your community.

Over the past decade, the seven largest investment groups vastly extended their reach as they purchased financially troubled legacy companies that came on the market. In 2016, the largest investment firms owned papers in 42 states, up from 27 in 2004.

In total, the seven largest investment firms own 14 percent of all newspapers in the country. In a dozen or so states, they own between a fifth to as much as a third of all newspapers. Massachusetts ranks at the top of states with the most papers owned by the large investment entities—141. After Massachusetts come California (112), Illinois (94), Texas (82), Ohio (74), Pennsylvania (61), New York (42), Florida (40), North Carolina (40) and Oklahoma (35). The large investment firms do not currently own local newspapers in eight states—Hawaii, Idaho, Montana, South Dakota, Vermont, Washington, Wisconsin and Wyoming. However, they do have a presence in several of these states since they also publish regional and statewide business journals and special-interest newspapers and magazines.

See newspaperownership.com/additional-material/ for a state-by-state listing of the number of papers owned by largest investment firms.

**WHERE THE LARGEST INVESTMENT COMPANIES OWNED NEWSPAPERS: 2004**

**WHERE THE LARGEST INVESTMENT COMPANIES OWNED NEWSPAPERS: 2016**

In 2004, the 3 largest investment companies owned 352 newspapers in 27 states.

SOURCE: UNC Database

In 2016, the 7 largest investment companies owned 1,031 newspapers in 42 states.

SOURCE: UNC Database

See newspaperownership.com/map/ to see where investment companies owned newspapers in 2004 and 2016.

Investment groups are most prevalent in New England, the Middle Atlantic, the South and the Pacific Coast regions. New England has experienced rapid growth in the number of papers owned by investment firms. In 2004, there were no investment firms in the region. By 2016, these firms owned 167, or 33 percent of all papers. Investment entities also had a significant presence in the Midwest, with 290 papers, and in the South, where they own 374 papers.

## WHERE THE LARGEST INVESTMENT COMPANIES OWN NEWSPAPERS: 2016

NEW MEDIA/GATEHOUSE    DIGITAL FIRST    CNHI    TRONC/TRIBUNE
CIVITAS    BH MEDIA GROUP    10/13 COMMUNICATIONS

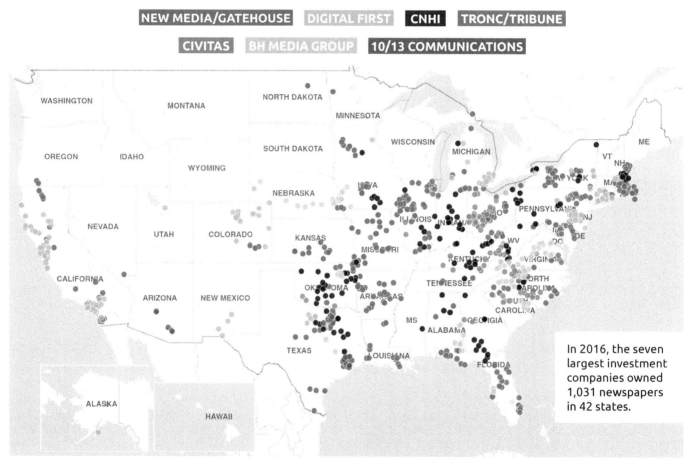

In 2016, the seven largest investment companies owned 1,031 newspapers in 42 states.

SOURCE: UNC Database

See newspaperownership.com/map/ to see where investment-owned newspapers are located.

## PERCENTAGE OF PAPERS OWNED BY INVESTMENT COMPANIES IN EACH REGION: 2004 & 2016

2004    2016

| | PACIFIC | MOUNTAIN | MIDWEST | SOUTH | MID-ATLANTIC | NEW ENGLAND |
|---|---|---|---|---|---|---|
| 2004 | 1% | 1% | 6% | 5% | 3% | 0% |
| 2016 | 17% | 6% | 10% | 15% | 13% | 33% |

**Pacific:** AK, CA, HI, OR, WA; **Mountain:** AZ, CO, ID, MT, NV, NM, UT, WV; **Midwest:** IL, IN, MI, OH, WI, IA, KS, MN, MO, NE, ND, SD;
**Mid-Atlantic:** NJ, NY, PA; **South:** DE, DC, FL, GA, MD, NC, SC, VA, WV, AL, KY, MS, TN, AR, LA, OK, TX; **New England:** CT, ME, MA, NH, RI, VT
SOURCE: UNC Database

## INVESTMENT-OWNED NEWSPAPERS BY REGION: 2016

| | Pacific | Mountain | Midwest | South | Mid-Atlantic | New England |
|---|---|---|---|---|---|---|
| New Media/GateHouse | 13 | 5 | 130 | 110 | 37 | 137 |
| Digital First | 87 | 20 | 21 | 13 | 47 | 20 |
| CNHI | 0 | 0 | 32 | 71 | 14 | 8 |
| Civitas | 0 | 0 | 44 | 41 | 5 | 44 |
| tronc/Tribune | 16 | 0 | 44 | 41 | 1 | 2 |
| BH Media | 0 | 0 | 19 | 58 | 3 | 0 |
| 10/13 Communications | 0 | 5 | 0 | 40 | 0 | 0 |

SOURCE: UNC Database

Each investment company has a distinctive geographic profile. The largest two, New Media and Digital First, own papers throughout the country. Others, like 10/13 Communications, are more narrowly focused on a specific region of the country. Here is a rundown:

**New Media/GateHouse** has a strong presence in New England, with 137 papers in Massachusetts, clustered in and around the greater Boston area, as well as in Illinois, with 36 papers, and in Ohio, with 30. For the most part, New Media has acquired papers in smaller markets not covered by regional television stations. The 125 daily papers owned by New Media/GateHouse have an average circulation of 14,500, and its nondaily papers have an average of 5,900.

**Digital First** owns 87 papers in the Pacific region, 85 of which are in California, clustered around the Bay Area in the North and around Los Angeles in the South. It also has 47 papers in the Middle Atlantic states, with 38 located in Pennsylvania. Digital First tends to own papers in mid-sized markets located in or near metro areas. The average circulation of its dailies is just under 34,000 and its nondailies, 13,200.

**Community Newspaper Holdings (CNHI)**, the pension-fund entity, has 20 newspapers in Oklahoma, 17 in Indiana and 12 in Kentucky. It tends to focus on small markets outside major metro areas. Its dailies have an average circulation of about 10,000 and and its nondailies, 7,500.

**Civitas** papers are clustered in the Midwest and South, including 41 papers in Ohio and 15 in North Carolina. As with CNHI, almost all of Civitas' papers—whether daily or nondaily—are located in small, rural markets. Its dailies have an average circulation of 9,800 and its nondailies, 6,700.

**tronc/Tribune** newspapers are located in eight major metro markets in seven states, including California, Illinois and Maryland. Tribune typically owns the major metro daily in each market and in recent years has focused on purchasing weeklies in nearby suburbs. It has 42 papers in Illinois—all in the greater Chicago metro area, 23 in Maryland in the Baltimore and Annapolis areas, and 15 in southern and central Florida, including Orlando and Fort Lauderdale. The average circulation of its 19 dailies is 108,000, and for its 85 weeklies it is 16,200.

**BH Media** papers are clustered in mid-sized markets in the South, including 26 papers in south-central Virginia and 11 in adjacent counties in north-central North Carolina, as well as the Midwest. It has 14 in Nebraska, including Omaha, the flagship paper. Its 32 dailies have an average circulation of 28,700, while its nondailies average 7,900.

**10/13 Communications**, the newest investment firm, owns 42 weeklies and three dailies—all located in or around Dallas and Houston in Texas and Phoenix and Tucson in Arizona. The average circulation of its papers is 19,000.

WHAT INVESTMENT COMPANIES LOOK FOR

Over the past decade, large investment entities acquired a large number of newspapers
in rural communities and/or economically struggling regions of the country.

From 2004 to 2016, the big seven acquired 1,004 newspapers—303 dailies and 701 nondailies. Nearly half of the papers purchased by investment firms had print circulation under 5,000, including a fifth of the dailies.

Investment firms acquired twice as many newspapers—257—in rural counties than either of large either public or private companies. This report uses the definition of rural in the U.S. Department of Agriculture's Rural-Urban Continuum Codes. Almost 60 percent of the papers owned by Civitas and CNHI, and 30 percent of the papers owned by BH Media and New Media/GateHouse, serve rural areas.

Forty percent—or 410—of the newspapers purchased by investment firms are located in counties with poverty rates at least 1 percentage point higher than the national rate of 14.8 percent. As a comparison, 217 of the purchases made by the largest 15 private chains and 104 purchases by the three public firms were in economically distressed areas. Between a half and two-thirds of the 340 papers currently owned by BH Media, 10/13, Civitas and CNHI are in counties with above-average poverty rates. About a third of the 753 papers owned by the other three large investment firms are in economically distressed areas.

Seventeen percent—or 86—of the newspapers owned by investment firms in the UNC database appear to be the only newspapers in the county where they are located. This raises the possibility that the lone newspapers in those counties have a de facto monopoly on local advertising, with an ability to set rates and conditions for readers and advertisers. Additionally, they are most likely the prime—if not only—source of local news and information.

### TYPE OF NEWSPAPER ACQUIRED: 2004–2016

| | Daily | Nondaily | Total | % in Impoverished Counties |
|---|---|---|---|---|
| New Media/ GateHouse | 130 | 313 | 443 | 39% |
| Digital First | 82 | 149 | 231 | 30% |
| CNHI | 11 | 9 | 20 | 35% |
| Civitas | 35 | 63 | 98 | 60% |
| tronc/Tribune | 8 | 58 | 66 | 39% |
| BH Media | 32 | 49 | 81 | 53% |
| 10/13 Communications | 3 | 44 | 47 | 62% |

The investment firms tended to acquire
small papers in impoverished areas.
SOURCE: UNC Database

The strategies that investment companies pursue tend to focus on short-term financial progress, not the long-term civic needs of the communities where their papers are located.

In inner cities and rural areas, the community newspaper historically has served as the prime source of reporting and commentary that could inform public policy decision-making.

The legacy chains of the late 20th century tended to "buy and hold" properties, and the most civic-minded also invested in aggressive and costly public service journalism.[72] The publishers and editors understood that the fortunes of the community and the newspaper were tightly linked. Publishers, even those hired by chain headquarters somewhere else, regularly took on civic engagement activities in the community of the newspaper they led.

The largest investment companies bring a different philosophy and day-to-day operational strategy. While the websites of the investment-owned newspapers still stress their civic mission and their aspirations to provide reliable and meaningful information to their communities, the public statements by executives of the large investment firms emphasize business and return on investment. See newspaperownership.com/additional-material/ for examples of public statements made by executives on why they purchase newspapers, their stated financial goals and their civic mission.

The rapid expansion of investment firms as newspaper owners occurs at the very moment newspapers are struggling to adapt to the digital era, with survival at stake. Advertising revenues, which historically provided more than 80 percent of total revenue for most local newspapers, have fallen to unprecedented levels and continue to decline as local and regional merchants shift spending to digital outlets.

When a mature industry is in decline, managers essentially have three options: *grow, maintain the status quo or "manage the decline"*:

- To *grow*, newspaper owners need to invest in both the business and news operations so they attract digital advertisers and readers. This long-term strategy requires owners to have faith in the future, an abiding commitment to the overarching mission of the paper and patience with the inevitable monthly and yearly financial fluctuations that come with charting a new direction.
- Newspaper owners can attempt to *maintain current profit margins* by cutting costs to keep pace with revenue declines while making minimal investments in digital products and services. This is a strategy of treading water, waiting for other newspapers to "crack the code" before committing to long-term investment.[73]
- Or newspaper owners can *manage the decline*, harvesting as much revenue as possible—usually by raising the rates charged advertisers and the subscription price to readers, and then either selling, trading or shutting down the newspaper as it becomes less profitable.

The investment firms do not air their operational decision-making. The fateful choices they make in the day-to-day management of small papers do not get attention outside the affected communities. Nevertheless, it is possible to identify common trends and strategies from corporate press releases and statements, as well as news accounts published in recent years. Investment firms have tended to pursue strategies that attempt to *maintain the status quo* and current profit margins—or, alternatively, *manage the decline* before either selling or shuttering unprofitable papers.

**Here are the major trends that have emerged:**

**A willingness to sell or close underperforming newspapers.** Investment firms are continually adjusting their portfolios to maximize financial return. Whenever possible, they attempt to sell or trade their underperforming newspapers to other chains or to local owners. Often the papers are purchased by other investment groups. For example, Heartland Publications, backed by Wachovia Capital Partners, was acquired in 2011 in bankruptcy proceedings by Versa Capital, owner of Civitas.

More than 300 papers owned by the largest investment firms have been sold or traded since 2004, according to news accounts and analysis of the UNC database. Relatively few newspapers were sold in the years immediately after the recession of 2008–2009, but sales have picked up since 2013. New Media/GateHouse, CNHI and Digital First have been the most active sellers in recent years. In the first week of August 2016, New Media/GateHouse, for example, sold 12 of its Illinois papers to Paddock Publishing at the same time it purchased The Fayetteville (North Carolina) Observer.

The turnover in staff that often occurs with the buying and flipping of properties erodes the connection of a local newspaper to the community. But at least there is still a newspaper. When no buyer can be found, investment entities are willing to close local newspapers.

The largest investment firms have closed or merged at least 85 newspapers, including 22 dailies, in the UNC database since 2004. New Media/GateHouse has closed or merged at least 40 papers and CNHI, 24. Since 2011, when Digital First, Civitas and BH Media were formed, these three investment firms have closed or merged 22 of their newspapers, including six dailies. The closed and merged dailies have had circulations ranging from 8,000 — the Kansas City Kansan, owned by New Media/GateHouse — to about 100,000 — the four San Francisco-area newspapers owned by Digital First that were merged to form the East Bay Times and South Bay Times.

**Establishment of an annual target for profit margins.** According to an Associated Press story, Warren Buffett said at the 2013 Berkshire Hathaway shareholder meeting that he expects "10 percent returns from the newspapers owned by BH Media every year," even though he also expects newspaper earnings to continue declining.[74]

While not revealing the profit margin of his small papers, Michael Bush, then CEO of Civitas, told an industry gathering in 2012, "The pessimism of others leads to understated valuations, which will improve over time as we prove the sustainability of current levels of profitability." He attributed his company's financial success to an emphasis on such short-term tactics as "increasing rate, as opposed to volume, on both advertising and circulation."[75]

In a 2014 prospectus provided to potential buyers, Digital First listed its profit margin in the 10 to 12 percent range. When no purchaser stepped forward, Digital First pursued a new round of cost-cutting designed to raise the profit margin, possibly as high as 20 percent.[76]

**A blurring of the line between the local newspaper's responsibility to readers and advertisers.** In May 2016, Tribune announced the combining of the jobs of publisher and editor at all its newspapers. Editors became publishers, responsible for the business operations as well as news gathering.[77]

A manager's handbook, written by the CEO of 10/13 Communications, explicitly stated that the primary focus of its newspapers should be pleasing the advertisers, not the readers: "Our customer is the advertiser. Readers are our customers' customers. [Therefore] we operate with a lean newsroom staff. … Sales are the lifeblood of the company…so it is clear that the top priority of all our newspapers is the sales department. Staffing should be as high as possible in sales and as low as possible in all other areas."[78]

**An increased willingness to declare bankruptcy.**
Four of the investment firms—New Media, Tribune, Civitas and Digital First—have filed for bankruptcy and financial restructuring over the past decade. All are either currently owned, or have been owned recently, by private equity or hedge funds, which still hold significant ownership stakes. A recent Columbia University study of private equity firms concluded, "If you're a large private equity firm, you own a diverse portfolio of companies. You don't need all of them to be successful…Because they [are] diversified, they're willing to take more risk. A family will do as much as possible to save the company, but for a PE firm, it doesn't matter as much. We find that private companies owned by PE firms tend to default more than similar public companies."[79]

**A lack of commitment to the communities their newspapers have historically served.** Because they have large and diverse portfolios of businesses, as well as dozens of newspapers, investment firms can allow individual papers to fail and still profit from their total holdings. When announcing that New Media/GateHouse planned to close 10 community weeklies in the Boston area, CEO Kirk Davis told the Boston Globe, "Business conditions have become more challenging, and it's more important to be selective about where you're putting the greatest amount of resources. We're going to shift resources to the highest potential markets that are most desirable to our advertisers."[80]

**Reliance on cost-cutting to achieve profit expectations, with diminished investment in the news operation.** "A lot of these companies are… looking for underperforming assets," says a media industry analyst for the research company Ibis World. "They'll acquire the local newspapers and they'll go in and slash operations to where these newspapers are profitable. It's kind of like flipping houses."[81]

While the websites of many newspapers owned by investment firms profess a commitment to "serving the community" through their journalism, their parent owners do not typically highlight this in their shareholder letters or public statements, instead emphasizing that they have moved quickly to "streamline" operations. Cost-cutting takes a variety of forms, including layoff of staff, wage freezes that extend for five or more years, unpaid furloughs and consolidation of news, advertising and circulation functions into regional centers that serve several papers. According to press accounts and various blogs, newspapers purchased by investment firms have experienced layoffs of between 10 and 40 percent of staff. In some cases, newspapers had already cut staff before the purchase by investment firms.

- Civitas notes that it has achieved "significant cost synergies by streamlining and consolidating" the advertising, circulation and news functions of its papers into regional centers.[82]
- New Media/GateHouse established a center in Austin, Texas, in 2013, to handle the editing and design of 175 newspapers. The center also produces original syndicated and sponsored content.[83]
- As part of an effort to save $100 million in costs, Digital First closed Thunderdome, an all-digital national newsroom established in 2013 to produce content for its 75 daily newspapers. It laid off the 50 "digital" journalists working there. Since 2011, Digital First has moved to consolidate the news and business operations of its 10 newspapers in the San Francisco Bay area. The most recent consolidation in 2015 was expected to result in another 20 percent news-staff reduction.[84]

**Less emphasis on expensive public service and accountability journalism.** In newsrooms with diminished staffing and often low morale, editors have to make day-to-day judgments about how to deploy limited resources. Do reporters cover stories that will "trend" and "engage readers"—as executives at New Media, Digital First and Tribune expect—or spend time on complex, time-consuming reporting that may or may not bear fruit? Do newspapers publish stories that may result in lawsuits and legal fees that diminish profits?

Even if they receive the green light from corporate headquarters, editors still must be selective about which stories their staffs ultimately pursue. With fewer reporters, these papers pursue fewer complicated stories. At the daily papers owned by Civitas, average circulation of 9,800, the one or two reporters only have time to focus on coverage of meetings and larger events in the community. When a major issue surfaces—typically at a city council or county commissioner meeting—there is rarely an editorial that advocates or takes a stand. In the space typically devoted to staff-written editorials, Civitas prints "letters to the editor," including the weekly constituent letters from the district's congressman.

**Lack of investment in the digital transformation:** While New Media, Digital First and Tribune are pushing newsrooms and advertising staffs to go digital, Civitas, CNHI and BH Media are moving more slowly and continuing to stress the importance of the print edition. Given the rapid adoption of smart phones by all age groups—even in rural areas—this may ultimately spell the demise of the papers owned by these companies.[85]

An examination of the media landscapes in Massachusetts, Illinois, Ohio, North Carolina, Kentucky and West Virginia offers insight into where and how ownership of newspapers has shifted dramatically over the past decade. And these six state profiles suggest the potential for news deserts to emerge in hard-hit rural and low-income regions of the country. Each of these states has regions tied to declining manufacturing, mining and farming.

Illinois, Ohio and North Carolina rank among the 10 most populous states. Still, more than half of their counties are classified by the U.S. Department of Agriculture as rural, many of them dealing with above-average unemployment, above-average poverty rates, an aging population, as well as health care and education issues. Regions of Kentucky and West Virginia, especially where investment firms own most or all of the papers, have some of the highest rates of poverty and unemployment in the country. Kentucky, West Virginia and Ohio are also faced with mounting environmental and ecological issues.

In Massachusetts, investment firms own two-thirds of all newspapers in the state. In the other five states, they now control at least a fifth of all papers. The communities in these states need their newspapers to provide the sort of public service journalism that can document and help identify solutions to their most pressing problems.

## MASSACHUSETTS: 2016

**NEW MEDIA/GATEHOUSE** **CNHI** **DIGITAL FIRST**

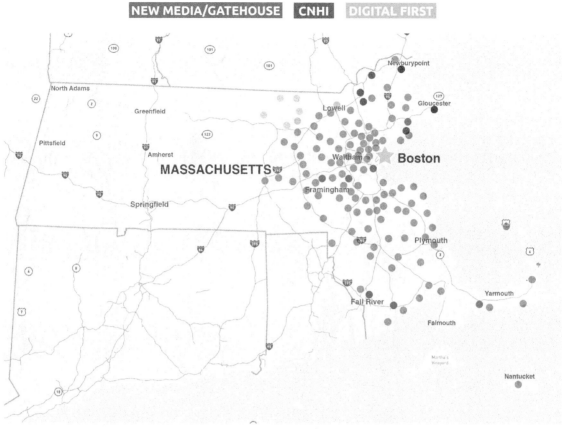

SOURCE: UNC Database

**State Overview:** Massachusetts is the 14th-most-populous state, with 6.7 million people. Seventy percent of the population is located in the state's eastern half. While Massachusetts enjoys higher household income and relatively lower unemployment rates than the national average, it faces a number of looming issues, including outdated transportation infrastructure, drug abuse especially in low-income urban areas, funding shortages for public education and an aging population with health care needs.[86] Additionally, in a recent analysis of the fiscal solvency of each of the 50 states, Massachusetts ranked 49th because of projected budget shortfalls related to underfunded state pension plans and imminent debt obligations.[87]

**Newspaper Ownership:** Of 226 papers in the state, 141 are owned by three investment entities, all purchased since 2004 and largely clustered in the greater Boston metro area and on Cape Cod.

By far, the dominant player in this market is New Media/GateHouse, which owns 126 papers (nine dailies and 117 nondailies), or 56 percent of the papers in the entire state and more than two-thirds of the papers in the populous eastern region.

Community Newspaper Holdings (CNHI) entered the state first by purchasing 10 papers in the northern Boston suburbs in 2005 from the privately held Eagle Tribune Publishing Co., headquartered in North Andover. In 2006, the New Media/GateHouse enterprise, which had just been acquired by Fortress Investment Group, bought 126 small nondaily papers in the Boston area from Community Newspaper Co. (not the same as CNHI) and rebranded these as WickedLocal. Digital First entered the state last in 2011 when it purchased the MediaNews chain in bankruptcy proceedings and acquired 11 newspapers in Massachusetts, including a daily in Lowell, northwest of Boston, and two other dailies in the middle of the state.

## LARGEST NEWSPAPER OWNERS IN MASSACHUSETTS

**Company Type:** Investment  Private

| Rank | Company | Total Papers | Daily Papers | Total Circ. (000s) | Daily Circ. (000s) |
|------|---------|--------------|--------------|--------------------|--------------------|
| 1 | New Media/GateHouse | 126 | 9 | 629 | 158 |
| 2 | Turley Publications | 10 | 0 | 74 | 0 |
| 3 | Digital First Media | 9 | 2 | 56 | 30 |
| 4 | Independent Newspaper Group (MA) | 8 | 0 | 62 | 0 |
| 5 | CNHI | 6 | 4 | 80 | 70 |

SOURCE: UNC Database

Since 2006, New Media/GateHouse has added to its Massachusetts empire by buying 13 newspapers from Enterprise News Media and five from the Dow Jones Local Media Group. Most recently, it acquired the Telegram & Gazette in Worcester, with 68,000 circulation, the third-largest daily in the state behind The Boston Globe and Boston Herald. The Worcester paper has changed ownership four times since 2013, when The New York Times Co. sold it to John Henry, owner of the Boston Red Sox, who then flipped it to Halifax Media. New Media then acquired the Halifax chain in 2015.

New Media/GateHouse CEO Kirk Davis told The Boston Globe in 2013 that the company's "history in Massachusetts is built around a mapping strategy in which covering a broad swath of the area's geography was paramount..." because GateHouse "wanted to be able to offer that market in combination buys" to local advertisers.[88]

While New Media's reach in the Boston metro area has extended significantly in recent years, the circulation of The Boston Globe has dropped. Since 2004, weekday circulation of The Globe, which The New York Times Co. in 2013 sold to John Henry, has declined to 230,000 in 2016, from 450,000. As a result, the combined 235,000 circulation of the nine dailies owned by New Media is comparable to that of the weekday Globe. And the total 629,000 circulation of all New Media papers—including 117 weeklies—is significantly more than the 365,000 Sunday circulation of The Globe.

(See newspaperownership.com/additional-material/ for list of papers owned by the largest investment groups in Massachusetts.)

**Looking Ahead:** The greater Boston market is now virtually divided between two newspaper companies. The Boston Globe owns the city and the greater metro area on a daily basis while New Media/GateHouse owns the suburbs with its collection of weeklies. The Globe can cover the major news that affects the region and provide context and analysis on statewide issues. But it doesn't have the reporting staff to cover the very local issues and concerns in each of its many suburbs. That responsibility falls to the editors of the weeklies owned by New Media/GateHouse. Yet the CEO of New Media has indicated the company's "mapping strategy" prioritizes the needs of the advertisers, not readers. When New Media/GateHouse shut down 10 Boston area weeklies in 2013, CEO Davis noted that the company was "shifting resources" to communities that local advertisers wanted to reach.[89] At the same time New Media continues to streamline and consolidate its news operations, leaving some of its communities to be covered by reporters from remote locations. In March 2016, GateHouse closed the Somerville newsroom, which was home to the Cambridge Chronicle and the Somerville Journal, and laid off the managing editor of the Boston-area newspapers. The 170-year-old Chronicle, the country's oldest continually published weekly, is now run out of the Lexington office, 22 miles away.[90] In a metro area as large and populated as Boston, the absence of reporters in the communities such as Cambridge suggests that many important stories will remain uncovered and unwritten.

## ILLINOIS: 2016

NEW MEDIA/GATEHOUSE   TRONC/TRIBUNE
CNHI   CIVITAS

SOURCE: UNC Database

**State Overview:** Illinois is the fifth-most-populous state, with 12.8 million people, yet, 62 of its 102 counties are classified as rural. Twenty-four of those counties have above-average rates of poverty. The state unemployment rate averaged 6.2 percent, compared with the national average of 4.9 in June 2016. Unemployment remains as high as 10 percent in some southern and western counties. Chicago's Cook County, with a poverty rate of 17.1 percent, has one of the highest violent crime rates in the country. Like Massachusetts, Illinois has projected short-term and long-term budget shortfalls, related to state pension and debt obligations. There are currently major political debates around proposals to raise property taxes in the wealthier Chicago suburbs and to open up more areas in the state for gambling and casinos.

**Newspaper Ownership:** Investment firms own 83 of the 477 newspapers in the state and control circulation of 1.1 million, 25 percent of total print circulation in Illinois. Investment firms staked out a presence earlier in Illinois than in most other states. In 1998, Leonard Green & Partners LP, a Los Angeles-based private equity firm, financed Liberty Publishing Group's purchase of 160 small papers in the upper Midwest from Hollinger International, including 70 in Illinois. Based in the Chicago suburb of Downers Grove, Liberty Publishing rapidly added to its holdings, doubling in size before downsizing to 250 papers in 2005, when it was purchased for $527 million by the New York-based private equity company Fortress Investment Group.[91] Fortress moved the headquarters to New York and renamed the company GateHouse. Since filing for bankruptcy reorganization in 2013, GateHouse is now known as New Media. Today, New Media, which owns more than 400 papers in 32 states, and Tribune Publishing, which was sold to a private equity firm in 2007, are the two dominant newspaper-owning investment firms in Illinois.

### LARGEST NEWSPAPER OWNERS IN ILLINOIS

Company Type: Public Investment Private

| Rank | Company | Total Papers | Daily Papers | Total Circ. (000s) | Daily Circ. (000s) |
|------|---------|--------------|--------------|--------------------|--------------------|
| 1 | Shaw Media | 80 | 7 | 425 | 77 |
| 2 | tronc/Tribune | 42 | 6 | 773 | 669 |
| 3 | New Media/ GateHouse | 34 | 13 | 298 | 167 |
| 4 | Southwest Messenger Press | 14 | 0 | 148 | 0 |
| 5 | Lee Enterprises | 12 | 5 | 201 | 78 |

SOURCE: UNC Database

In the past four years, a significant realignment of newspaper ownership has taken place in the greater Chicago metro area, with a population of 9.5 million. Four major owners—New Media, Tribune, Shaw Media and the Sun-Times—have either purchased or divested assets. In 2012, New Media retreated entirely from the Chicago market, selling all its suburban weeklies to the private, family-owned Shaw Media Co., founded in 1851. As a result, Shaw, which is based in the Chicago suburb of Dixon and owns 80 newspapers, became the dominant media provider in the outer western suburbs, with a total circulation in the greater metro area of 436,000.

Two years after Shaw purchased the suburban papers from New Media, the Tribune Publishing Co. acquired from the Chicago Sun-Times 36 papers—four dailies and 32 weeklies—located in four counties of the inner Chicago metro area: Cook, Lake, DuPage and Kane. In purchasing these suburban papers, the Tribune Co. positioned itself to provide print and digital marketing services to local and national advertisers who want to reach either the entire metro area or to target specific suburban communities. As a press release put it, the company's footprint spans "from Waukegan [in the north] to northwest Indiana" in the south.[92] The combined daily and weekly circulation of 773,000 of the Tribune papers is greater than any other publication in Illinois and dwarfs the Sun-Times' circulation of 210,000.

With the greater Chicago market split for the moment between Shaw and tronc/Tribune, New Media has focused its attention on its other newspapers, most of which are in rural southern and western Illinois. In August 2016, it sold 11 papers, including five dailies, in southern counties to the privately owned Paddock Publications. New Media now owns only 34 papers, including 13 dailies, most clustered in rural western and central Illinois. This includes the three largest dailies outside Chicago: the Peoria Journal Star, with circulation 58,500; the Rockford Register Star, with 53,500; and The State Journal-Register in Springfield, with 44,000. Most of the other 33 New Media papers are under 10,000 circulation. Seven of the 22 counties in which New Media now owns a paper—including the three where the large dailies are located—have above-average poverty and unemployment rates. In nine of the state's counties, New Media owns all the papers, making it the sole provider of local news and advertising.

(See newspaperownership.com/additional-material/ for list of papers owned by the largest investment groups in Illinois.)

**Looking Ahead:** While New Media has a long history in Illinois, dating back to the founding of Liberty Publishing Co. in 1998, its future there is less certain. New Media has been willing to divest properties with sluggish revenue and profit, or those that do not align with the company's regional advertising strategies. Since 2012, it has sold half of its Illinois papers—to Shaw and, most recently, to Paddock—raising the question of what the future holds for the remaining New Media newspapers and the communities where those papers are located.

Similarly, the future of the Tribune-owned papers in the Chicago market is far from certain. The company has emerged from bankruptcy still saddled with significant debt. Numerous changes in management have occurred over the past decade as the company went through several financial restructurings and corporate reorganizations. Various strategies have been tried and discarded. The purchase of the suburban papers was orchestrated by the previous CEO, Jack Griffin, who was ousted in early 2016 by the principal investor, Michael Ferro, who is now fighting a hostile takeover bid from Gannett and pressure from the Tribune's creditors to sell.[93]

## OHIO: 2016

CIVITAS · NEW MEDIA/GATEHOUSE · CNHI · DIGITAL FIRST

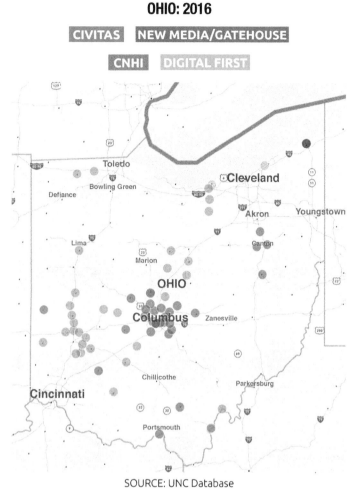

SOURCE: UNC Database

**State Overview:** Ohio is the seventh-most-populous state, with 11.6 million people. Of its 143 counties, 84 are rural, and 39 have poverty rates above the national average. In recent times, it has been a bellwether "swing state" in presidential elections. Currently, the most animated debates on public policy in Ohio revolve around drug addiction and crime, the quality of public education, taxation as it relates to economic development, and fracking regulations and pollution of the Great Lakes.[94] Ohio is also one of the older-population states, with a median age of almost 40.

**Newspaper Overview:** Investment firms own 74 of the state's 300 newspapers and control 22 percent of the 3.9 million total circulation. Two investment firms, New Media Investment Group and Civitas, own 71 papers between them.

GateHouse, the predecessor of New Media, entered the market in 2007 with its purchase of five papers from Copley Press, the largest being the 55,000-circulation daily The Repository in Canton, south of Cleveland and Akron.[95] Until recently, New Media has focused on purchasing papers in smaller markets. But since emerging from bankruptcy in 2013, the firm has opportunistically purchased papers in larger markets.[96] New Media purchased the Providence (Rhode Island) Journal for $46 million in 2014, and in 2015, it paid $47 million cash and for the second-largest paper in Ohio, the family-owned Columbus Dispatch, with a circulation of 134,000.[97]

Press releases issued by New Media when it purchased the Columbus and Providence papers note that both cities are "capitals of government and commerce," and, as such, are "attractive regional advertising markets." With the addition of the Columbus daily and the 24 weeklies owned by the Dispatch Co., New Media has circulation of 472,000 in Ohio, compared with the 594,000 circulation of Advance Publications, which owns the state's largest newspaper, The Plain Dealer in Cleveland, as well as 12 other newspapers in the state. In central and eastern Ohio, New Media has a largely uncontested claim on an attractive regional advertising market that, for the most part, enjoys below-average rates of poverty and unemployment.

### LARGEST NEWSPAPER OWNERS IN OHIO

**Company Type:** Public · Investment · Private

| Rank | Company | Total Papers | Daily Papers | Total Circ. (000s) | Daily Circ. (000s) |
|------|---------|--------------|--------------|--------------------|--------------------|
| 1 | Civitas Media | 41 | 16 | 327 | 156 |
| 2 | New Media/ GateHouse | 30 | 4 | 472 | 173 |
| 3 | Gannett | 27 | 11 | 327 | 157 |
| 4 | Dix Communications | 20 | 6 | 180 | 75 |
| 5 | Advance Publications | 13 | 1 | 594 | 312 |

SOURCE: UNC Database

Versa Capital Management, a Pennsylvania-based private equity firm, entered the Ohio market in 2011, purchasing 44 papers from Ohio Community Media, a holding company formed by creditors of Brown Publishing, a 90-year-old private, family-operated chain of small dailies and weeklies, based in Cincinnati, that had filed for bankruptcy.[98] In 2012, Versa added to its Ohio holdings by purchasing The Lima News from Freedom Communications and acquired Heartland Publications, a bankrupt newspaper chain located in the Southern states. Versa merged its two newspaper groups to form Civitas. After selling three papers and closing four others in 2014, the Civitas group owns papers in 22 counties in Ohio, mostly clustered in the less populated counties in the west, northwest and southeast. Twenty-nine of its remaining 41 newspapers have circulation below 10,000. Only five are above 20,000, and only three are dailies. They include the Community Common in Portsmouth, with a circulation of 35,000. The Community Common is located in Scioto County, population 80,000, on the Ohio River border with Kentucky, and has a poverty rate of 24.8 percent. Thirteen of the papers owned by Civitas are in counties with unemployment and poverty rates considerably above both the state and national rates. Civitas owns the only newspapers serving four of those economically struggling counties.

(See newspaperownership.com/additional-material/ for list of papers owned by the largest investment groups in Ohio.)

**Looking Ahead:** Investment firms own a quarter of all newspapers in Ohio. Still, other large public (Gannett) and private (Advance) chains also have a significant presence. Most of the major markets in the state are relatively self-contained, with very little competition from other newspapers — Advance in the Cleveland metro area, Gannett in Cincinnati, and New Media in Columbus. But while newspaper ownership in the metro areas appears relatively stable for now, the future of the newspapers in rural Ohio is less certain. Since 2012, Civitas (aka Versa) has closed three "underperforming" weeklies and one daily in four Ohio communities that were struggling economically — and no other news organization has stepped in to fill the void.

## NORTH CAROLINA: 2016

**CIVITAS**  **NEW MEDIA/GATEHOUSE**  **BH MEDIA GROUP**  **CNHI**

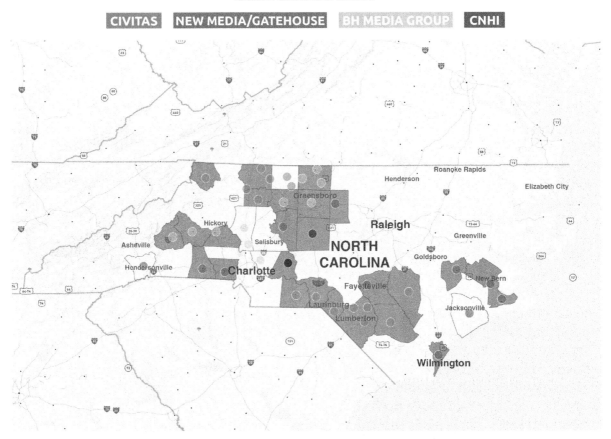

Counties that are shaded in gray have poverty rates above the national average.
SOURCE: UNC Database

**State Overview:** North Carolina, an increasingly important swing state in national elections, is the ninth-most-populous state, with 10 million people. Of its 100 counties, 56 are rural. While its major metro areas are generally thriving economically, 34 counties, mostly rural, have above-average rates of poverty and unemployment. The 2008–2009 recession cut sharply into textile and furniture manufacturing, depriving small towns of low-wage, but steady, employment. The state is facing several environmental issues, including the disposal of coal ash.[99]

**Newspaper Overview:** Investment firms own 40 of 185 papers and control 20 percent of the total circulation of 2.4 million. The two largest daily newspapers—The Charlotte Observer, with 107,000 circulation, and The News & Observer in Raleigh, with 94,000 circulation—are owned

by McClatchy. The next four largest dailies in the state are owned by BH Media and New Media/GateHouse. BH Media, a division of Berkshire Hathaway, owns the Winston-Salem Journal, with 60,000 circulation, and the News & Record in Greensboro, with 46,500 circulation, in the middle of the state. New Media/GateHouse owns The Fayetteville Observer, with 37,000 circulation, and the Star-News in Wilmington, with 36,000 circulation in the southeastern part of the state.

BH Media, Civitas and New Media Investment Group each own 10 or more newspapers in the state. All are newcomers. Civitas and BH Media entered North Carolina in 2012—Civitas by purchasing Heartland Publications in bankruptcy proceedings from another private equity firm and BH Media by purchasing the 10 newspapers in North Carolina owned by Media General, including the Winston-Salem Journal.[100] The New Media Investment group entered in late

## LARGEST NEWSPAPER OWNERS IN NORTH CAROLINA

Company Type: Public Investment Private

| Rank | Company | Total Papers | Daily Papers | Total Circ. (000s) | Daily Circ. (000s) |
|------|---------|--------------|--------------|--------------------|--------------------|
| 1 | Civitas Media | 15 | 5 | 113 | 60 |
| 2 | McClatchy | 12 | 2 | 697 | 202 |
| 3 | New Media/ GateHouse | 12 | 11 | 190 | 188 |
| 4 | BH Media | 11 | 6 | 167 | 137 |
| 5 | Cooke Communications | 11 | 3 | 81 | 40 |

SOURCE: UNC Database

2014 when it purchased the private Halifax chain, composed of newspapers in North Carolina that had previously been owned by The New York Times Co. and Freedom Communications.[101] In August 2016, New Media/Gatehouse purchased the oldest paper in the state, the 200-year-old, family-owned Fayetteville Observer, which covers Fort Bragg and nine rural—mostly poor—counties.[102]

These three investment firms have also acquired newspapers in counties with significantly above-average poverty rates. Civitas owns papers in nine of the poorest counties in the state, including three in the northwest and six along the U.S. 74 corridor in the southeast. In eight of those counties, Civitas is the sole newspaper proprietor. It has only two North Carolina newspapers with a circulation of more than 10,000: The Robesonian in Lumberton, with 10,800, and the Mount Airy News, with 10,620. Robeson County has a poverty rate of 33.1 percent, and Surry County, home of Mount Airy, has a poverty rate of 18.8 percent, both significantly above the 14.8 national average.

BH Media's 11 papers are in north-central North Carolina near Interstate 40. Eight are located in counties with above-average poverty rates, and in two of those counties, the firm owns all the area newspapers. New Media/GateHouse owns a collection of papers clustered mostly in the southeastern part of the state, stretching from Fayetteville to the coast, and along I-85 in the central part of the state. Nine of the 11 counties in which New Media owns papers have above-average poverty rates.

(See http://newspaperownership.com/additional-material/ for list of papers owned by the largest investment groups in North Carolina.)

**Looking Ahead:** Because they are relatively new to the state, it is too early to know whether BH Media, New Media/GateHouse and Civitas are "here to stay" in North Carolina or merely passing through. Warren Buffett is retiring as head of Berkshire Hathaway, and it's unknown whether his successors will match his interest in newspapers.[103] Over the last decade, New Media has continually adjusted its portfolio as it seeks to build regional advertising markets around its newspapers. With its purchase of the Fayetteville paper, New Media appears to be solidifying its hold on the southeastern portion of state. The five small papers in the central part of the state may not align with their regional advertising strategy and therefore might end up shut down or traded, most likely to either BH Media or Civitas, which already own papers in that area.

## KENTUCKY & WEST VIRGINIA: 2016

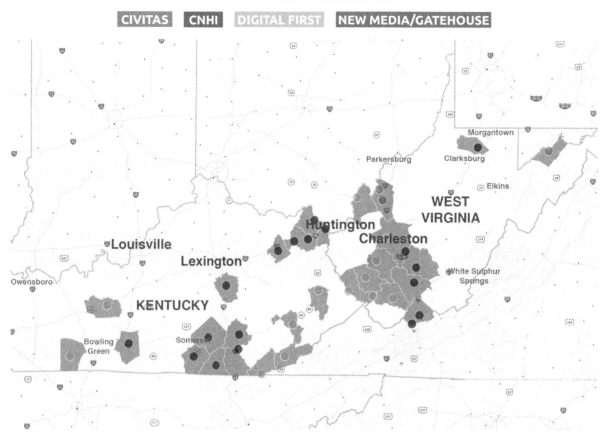

CIVITAS　CNHI　DIGITAL FIRST　NEW MEDIA/GATEHOUSE

Counties that are shaded in gray have poverty rates above the national average.
SOURCE: UNC Database

**State Overview:** Kentucky and West Virginia are among the least-densely populated states in the eastern U.S. and have similar challenges. Both are relatively rural and impoverished. Kentucky ranks 26th among the states, with a population of 4.4 million; West Virginia, which has 1.8 million people, is 38th. In Kentucky, 85 of 119 counties are classified as rural, and a third have above-average poverty rates. In West Virginia, 34 of 55 counties are rural, and three-quarters of the counties are struggling economically. The poorest counties tend to be in the Appalachian areas of both states and along the Ohio River. The most serious issues confronting both states include high unemployment, low education levels, drug abuse, long-term environmental damage and lack of funding to support public education, health care for an aging population and transportation infrastructure.[104]

**Newspaper Overview:** The percentage of newspapers owned by investment entities in Kentucky is a relatively low 12 percent. However, in the eastern counties of Kentucky and the adjoining southwestern portion of West Virginia, investment firms own more than half of 44 papers in those counties, some of the poorest

### LARGEST NEWSPAPER OWNERS IN KENTUCKY

Company Type: Public Investment Private

| Rank | Company | Total Papers | Daily Papers | Total Circ. (000s) | Daily Circ. (000s) |
|------|---------|--------------|--------------|--------------------|--------------------|
| 1 | Landmark Media Enterprises | 19 | 1 | 111 | 11 |
| 2 | CNHI | 12 | 5 | 76 | 34 |
| 3 | Gannett | 10 | 2 | 166 | 95 |
| 4 | Paxton Media Group | 9 | 4 | 71 | 52 |
| 5 | Civitas Media | 6 | 2 | 32 | 11 |

SOURCE: UNC Database

## LARGEST NEWSPAPER OWNERS IN WEST VIRGINIA

**Company Type:** Public Investment Private

| Rank | Company | Total Papers | Daily Papers | Total Circ. (000s) | Daily Circ. (000s) |
|------|---------|--------------|--------------|--------------------|--------------------|
| 1 | Ogden Newspapers | 7 | 5 | 63 | 53 |
| 2 | Civitas Media | 6 | 3 | 32 | 22 |
| 3 | CNHI | 6 | 3 | 47 | 38 |
| 4 | Moffitt Newspapers | 6 | 1 | 38 | 4 |
| 5 | New Media/ GateHouse | 4 | 1 | 22 | 4 |

SOURCE: UNC Database

in both states. In fact, *all* of the 35 papers in Kentucky and West Virginia owned by investment companies are located in counties with above-average poverty rates.

Community Newspaper Holdings owns 18 papers in the two states—12 in Kentucky, six in West Virginia. These were among the first papers acquired by CNHI when it was formed by the Retirement Systems of Alabama in the late 1990s. Only four of the papers owned by CNHI have circulation above 10,000—the largest being The Register-Herald in Beckley, West Virginia, with just over 20,000 in circulation.

Civitas acquired six papers in each state when it purchased the bankrupt Heartland Publications chain in 2012. All 12 papers owned by Civitas have circulation under 10,000. During the last decade, New Media/GateHouse also acquired four small West Virginia papers, all below 10,000 in circulation.

The three major regional papers in the two states have little readership in the areas where Civitas and CNHI own papers. The circulation of the Gannett-owned Louisville (Kentucky) Courier-Journal, the largest paper in either state, has dropped to 89,000 in 2016 from 207,000 in 2004. The McClatchy-owned Lexington Herald-Leader has dropped to 74,000 in circulation from 114,000. The Charleston (West Virginia) Gazette-Mail's circulation of 46,000 is predominantly in the metro area. In 18 of the 25 rural counties in which they have a presence, Civitas and CNHI own all the newspapers.

(See newspaperownership.com/additional-material/ for a list of papers owned by the largest investment groups in Kentucky and West Virginia.)

**Looking Ahead:** Privately held Landmark Media Enterprises, which owns 19 community papers in Kentucky, is the largest newspaper owner in the state. Since 2008, Landmark has sold off its Greensboro (North Carolina) News & Record and Roanoke (Virginia) papers to BH Media and its Annapolis (Maryland) paper to Tribune. Landmark has indicated that it intends to sell all its newspapers. If Landmark's Kentucky newspapers attract investment firms, the number of papers owned by investment firms would rise significantly. Conversely, CNHI, Civitas and New Media could decide to exit. Since 2012, those three firms have been among the most aggressive in shutting down and selling underperforming papers. In either scenario, the newspaper landscape in Kentucky and West Virginia likely will change dramatically in the near future—and the communities that will be most affected are the poorest.

The futures of newspapers owned by investment firms and the communities that these papers serve are inextricably linked. Both newspapers and rural communities are struggling to adapt technologically and financially to macro-economic change and the digital era. If the local newspaper fails, no other medium, such as television or radio, is capable of providing these communities with the sort of public service journalism that lays out the issues and holds public servants accountable.

Extensive research has found that local newspapers, more than any other medium, have an important agenda-setting function. They have the ability to shed light on community needs, to determine the major issues debated by citizens and to help point a community toward decisions on public policies.[105] By reporting important stories and giving prominence to them, editors and publishers of local papers set the agenda and contribute to the quality of life in their communities. Historically, many papers have also followed their reporting with editorials that argue for specific courses of action.

According to some estimates, newspapers provide as much as 85 percent of "the news that feeds democracy" at the local, state and national levels.[106] Without investment in journalism and digital technologies, the ability of local newspapers to survive as a credible voice for their communities in the 21st century is threatened.

A 2011 Federal Communications Commission report found that, absent a strong local newspaper, no other medium is positioned to step in with public service journalism that sheds light on the major issues confronting communities, large and small.[107]

**Regional or Metro Newspapers:** Several Pulitzer Prizes won by large daily papers in the latter half of the 20th century focused on regional issues that affected rural residents. The News & Observer of Raleigh, North Carolina, for example, received the Pulitzer Public Service award in 1996 for its series on industrial hog farming in eastern North Carolina. Since 2000, however, newsroom staffing across the country has dropped by almost 40 percent.[108] Some papers, like The News & Observer, which is owned by the McClatchy Co., have retained a

corps of investigative reporters, but there is ample documentation of a dramatic drop in coverage of city halls and statehouses. As advertising revenue plummeted, many metro papers pulled back distribution from outlying regions. Consequently, circulation of most large regional newspapers has declined 42 percent. With fewer reporters covering statewide or regional beats and fewer readers in outlying areas, metro papers give much less attention to issues uniquely affecting rural counties, many of which are struggling economically.

**Regional Television Stations:** Even though TV stations have expanded the daily time allotted to local news in many markets, the preponderance of those newscasts revolves around "soft" features, crime, human interest stories, weather, sports and scheduled events. The FCC report found that only 10 percent of airtime—under two and a half minutes—on an evening news show is typically devoted to discussing statewide and regional issues such as health care and education.[109] A 2009 study of a Los Angeles TV station found that, on average, only slightly more than one minute of a 30-minute evening broadcast covered local issues such as education, environment, health and transportation.[110] Most television stations, unlike newspapers, do not have an editorial voice that commands community attention. With few exceptions, regional television stations have fewer reporters than the dominant newspaper in the market. As a result, coverage beyond the core metro market is usually limited to the weather forecast, tornadoes, hurricanes and major accidents.

**Radio:** Fewer than 40 percent of U.S. residents live where they can receive all-news radio. While National Public Radio covers national, international and regional news, relatively few public radio stations provide extensive local reporting in small and mid-sized markets. Only 60 percent of commercial radio stations have even 30 minutes of local news a day, and this "newscast" often consists of a listing of upcoming events, along with an interview with a local official or celebrity. More than a fifth of all commercial radio stations have no local news at all.

**Nonprofit News Organizations:** Nonprofit news organizations have arisen as alternative sources of news that can potentially fill the gap created as local newspapers shrink. However, most nonprofit news organizations are located in metropolitan areas, and many are primarily online at a time when as many as half of residents in rural communities still lack reliable access to broadband or wireless services.[111] Of 172 nonprofit news outlets surveyed by the Pew Research Center in 2012, 101 focused on global, national or state news, and another 49 focused on metropolitan news.[112] Of the 13 hyperlocal sites, all but two were in large cities. Start-up nonprofit organizations also face their own financial challenges. A 2015 Knight Foundation survey of 20 organizations concluded that only a handful were on solid financial footing. The average nonprofit relied on support from philanthropic foundations for almost 60 percent of its annual operating budget. Only 20 percent came from earned income, such as sponsorships or advertising. Only six of the nonprofits had an annual surplus that could be tapped for emergencies.

## WHERE NONPROFIT NEWS ORGANIZATIONS WERE LOCATED: 2012

Number of Nonprofit News Sources  1 •  5 •  10 ●  14 ●

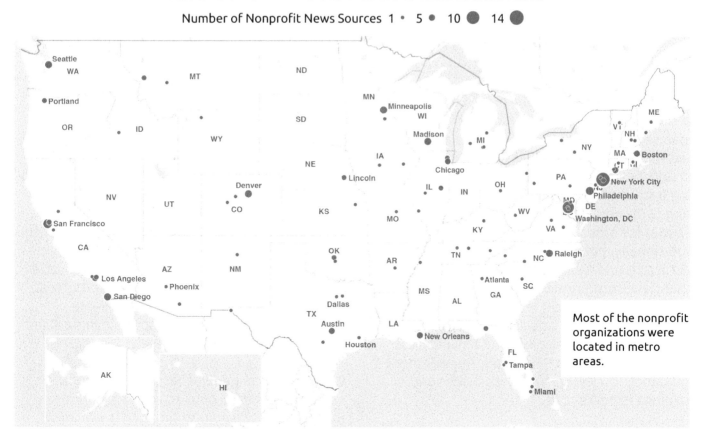

Most of the nonprofit organizations were located in metro areas.

SOURCE: Pew Research Center

A century ago, when Scripps and Hearst were assembling the first newspaper chains, more than nine out of 10 papers in the U.S. were independently owned and operated.[113] By 2000, nine out of 10 papers were links in a media chain. Throughout the 20th century, media critics raised concerns about the fiduciary responsibility of nonresident newspaper owners to the communities where their papers were located. Now, the rapid rise in newspapers owned by large investment companies poses a special set of issues in the digital age.

The late 20th century chain had to be attentive to shareholder needs and balance them against community needs. However, since most newspapers before 2008 sold for between 11 and 13 times yearly earnings, chain owners had a strong financial incentive to take a long-term view on investment and hold onto a paper for at least a decade and a half.[114] Additionally, publicly held companies, such as McClatchy and Gannett, are required to file financial information with government agencies, guaranteeing a certain level of transparency about management's decisions. Diligent shareholders can make informed investment decisions based on a newspaper management's "guidance" on its journalistic priorities and earnings expectations.

Unlike the publicly traded chains, investment groups can operate with almost no financial or management transparency. Nor do they automatically have a long-term commitment to a newspaper they have purchased. Investment firms have indicated they will sell or shut down underperforming or unprofitable papers without regard to the void left in the communities where the papers are located. As the number of papers they own balloons, they become more and more removed from the hundreds of communities in 42 states where they own papers. Taken together, these factors make it difficult for readers, advertisers and community leaders to hold the owners of their local paper accountable for the quality and quantity of news and information.

Low-income and rural communities need strong newspapers to give voice to their interests and concerns, provide context and analysis around problems and solutions, and help set the agenda for debate and adoption of effective public policies. Television and radio offer little more than spotty coverage; their intermittent attention does not make them a reliable alternative news sources for people in rural and low-income areas.

Without a local paper, there is a strong risk of news deserts emerging across vast regions in the country with communities that can least afford it—with political, economic and social consequences for society as a whole.

# COUNTIES WITH INVESTMENT OWNED NEWSPAPERS: 2016

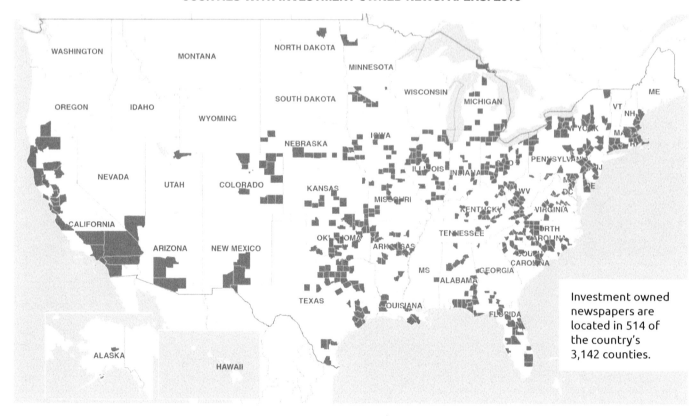

Investment owned newspapers are located in 514 of the country's 3,142 counties.

SOURCE: UNC Database

# FINDING SOLUTIONS:
# SAVING COMMUNITY JOURNALISM

Walter Lippmann, one of American's pre-eminent journalists and commentators in the 20th century, referred to a newspaper as "the bible of democracy, the book out of which a people determines its conduct."[115] Scholars have argued that strong local newspapers have the ability to "set the agenda" by determining the important public issues that a community debates and decides.[116] Modern-day economists refer to the journalism produced by newspapers as a public good. In theory, the better informed a community's citizens, the better they will be in making everyday decisions that could enhance their own and their neighbors' quality of life.

Over the past decade and a half, the newspaper industry has experienced unprecedented economic and technological disruption. Out of that caldron of instability, a new media baron has emerged—investment entities now own a growing number of newspapers across the country.

There is no guarantee newspapers will survive, especially if their owners do not possess *both* journalism's civic mission and the business savvy to discard old business models and create new ones. This is a classic moment, leaving all of us in society with challenging questions about the role of both newspapers and newspaper owners in the 21st century.

In an age of disruption and consolidation, the future of newspapers and communities throughout the country is at stake. In addition to newspaper owners, individuals and institutions will need to make a committed and concerted effort to save community journalism. Earlier, this report documented the dramatic shift in newspaper ownership and the emerging threat of "news deserts" developing in regions across the country. The concluding chapter attempts to identify interested parties and some actions they can take *now* to ensure that community newspapers—whether on paper or digitally—continue to provide news that feeds democracy at the local level. Far from an exhaustive list, what follows is intended to start a conversation at national and local levels before it is too late.

**The most urgent challenge for newspaper owners is developing new sources of digital revenue so they can survive and continue producing the news that feeds democracy.**

The disruption in the newspaper industry over the past decade is a textbook example of "creative destruction" when old ways of doing business fade and new models are created. In other industries that have experienced such massive economic disruption, survivors transformed their business models by aggressively cutting costs associated with the legacy product while simultaneously adopting the new technology so they could attract new customers and new sources of revenue.

Most newspapers have significantly cut costs related to their print edition, and many have invested in technology to reach readers anytime, anywhere. But the vast majority still remain almost totally dependent on rapidly declining print advertising revenue to pay the bills.

Several recent industry studies have found that there is enough digital advertising and marketing revenue in many markets, whether large or small, to support a robust local news gathering function.[117] However, community newspapers currently receive only a fraction of that revenue—many less than 5 percent. So even if local newspapers now owned by investment entities and other large legacy chains revert to local owners with a passion for civic journalism, these papers will most likely fail if the new owners do not develop new sources of revenue quickly.

To survive and thrive in the digital age, community newspapers need to transform their advertising departments and develop revenue strategies that more closely align with the marketing needs of their local businesses. This involves moving beyond mere sales of advertising space in one of the paper's print or digital editions and, instead, offering a full range of digital services, including search engine optimization, social media management, website design and video production. There will be much trial and error, as this is totally new territory for newspapers. What works in one market may not work in another, so strategies will need to be tailored to individual communities.

**Schools of journalism and communication** have historically focused on training current and future journalists, as well as public relations and advertising professionals. Many major schools have recently begun teaching students concepts and skills around "innovation and entrepreneurship." But while this focus may help them start their own businesses at some future date, it does not address the pressing business issues that community newspapers are currently experiencing. Newspaper owners—especially those in rural and low-income communities—need university faculty and students to produce applied research that assists them in developing and implementing new *and sustainable* business strategies, as well as tools for measuring progress against goals. UNC's Center for Innovation and Sustainability in Local Media is one example of university outreach and collaboration with both newspapers and communities. A soon-to-be-published white paper, for example, examines the feasibility of small newspapers in low-income areas establishing profitable full-service digital marketing agencies that fulfill the marketing needs of small businesses in the community.[118]

**Press associations** have historically served as effective lobbyists, working at the state and national level to preserve newspaper revenue from government-required legal notices, for example, or postal discounts. They have also fought aggressively for open meetings and public records laws. But a new emphasis is required. Legal ads, printed inserts and national ads are going the way of classified advertising. Industry analysts expect these three forms of print advertising to disappear from most community newspapers within the next five years.[119] Press associations need to work *now* with news organizations in planning for the future. Their primary focus needs to move from preservation of the status quo—lobbying state legislators to protect legal ad revenue for yet another year—to working with universities and newspaper owners to support research and development of business models and revenue strategies that allow newspapers to survive in the digital age.

**Governmental media policies** in the 20th century focused on keeping competitive newspapers "alive" through joint operating agreements, which ultimately didn't work. Federal policy also sought to prevent the owners of a traditional news organization, whether TV, radio or newspaper, from holding a cross-media local "monopoly." The measures the Federal Communications Commission and the Department of Justice use for determining media "concentration" in local markets are 20th-century contrivances and do not acknowledge the competition from new media that threatens all traditional media. The major digital competitors in most markets are now Facebook and Google.[120] What's more, a 2011 FCC report detailed how IRS rules constrain nonprofit organizations in developing new sources of revenue by limiting how much they can get from advertising.[121] IRS rules need to be revised so that nonprofit news organizations can also develop scalable and sustainable business models, instead of relying primarily on donations from individuals and foundations.

**Cutbacks in newsroom staffing have left many communities and regions in this country—especially those that are rural and less affluent—underserved by news media. Several hundred newspapers in the past decade have either ceased publishing or merged with other papers, leaving their communities without a media outlet.**

Too many newspapers still see other news organizations as competitors. In addition to developing new revenue strategies, newspapers also need to consider new models for reporting to ensure that underserved communities receive the news and information they need.

Newspapers in small and low-income communities—where the majority of investment-owned publications are located—are so understaffed that many struggle to cover routine events, such as town council meetings. And large metros, which have endured multiple rounds of layoffs, are not able to produce either the number or range of enterprise and investigative series that they did in the past.

Therefore, **newspaper publishers and editors** need to develop partnerships and networks with other news organizations that stress collaboration instead of competition. These networks can take many forms, uniting metro dailies with smaller weeklies, independent and chain-owned papers, or nonprofits and for-profit dailies.

Two recent journalistic endeavors by investment-owned newspapers illustrate that civic-minded editors—at both large and small papers—can rise to the challenge when they have the backing of corporate headquarters. Reporters at the Sarasota Herald-Tribune, owned by New Media/Gatehouse, worked collaboratively for a year with journalists at the independently owned Tampa Bay Times, detailing the increase in violence and abuse at state-run mental facilities after major cuts in funding.[122] The two papers shared the 2016 Pulitzer Prize for Investigative Reporting. At the same time, Community News Holdings (CNHI), the oldest of the large newspaper investment groups, founded almost 20 years ago, has been upgrading its coverage of state and regional issues in seven states where it has the largest number of papers, most with circulation under 10,000. CNHI has designated one journalist in each of those states to produce both regional enterprise stories and cover statehouse news about policy issues that affect the communities where its papers are located.[123]

Unfortunately, these two notable collaborative journalistic efforts remain the exception in the industry as a whole, and especially among the investment-owned papers. While supporting the public service journalistic endeavors of some papers, both New Media/Gatehouse and CNHI have simultaneously closed unprofitable papers in small, low-income communities. That is the risk as the large chains grow even larger; they can selectively support some papers and not others—unless all papers are key links in a greater network.

Similarly, locally owned independent news outlets, including newspapers, nonprofit online outlets and broadcasters, need to establish their own collaborative journalistic ventures and networks that allow them to both cover dig deeper into the many important public policy issues in their regions. Partnerships may also ultimately determine the ability of independent and nonprofit organizations to survive, since they are stronger together. As an example, public broadcasting stations in three states have banded together to form the Ohio River Network.[124]

**Large community and journalism-related foundations** have mostly funded nonprofit news organizations in major cities that have stepped in to fill the news and information gaps left by the decline of metropolitan newspapers. Though some attempt to report on education, health, environmental and economic issues of concern to distressed communities, most report on news that originates in metro areas. Now is the time for foundations to focus on areas that are in danger of becoming news deserts. They can make it imperative that those organizations that they do fund reach beyond "hyper-local coverage" in a specific metro area. And they can start funding nonprofits that provide "regional" contextual/analytical reporting. Examples in North Carolina include North Carolina Health News and EducationNC.

They can also encourage partnerships — between for-profit news organizations and nonprofits or between universities and nonprofits. Some universities are already partnering with local nonprofit startups to provide information to underserved communities. However, most of these partnerships focus their news coverage on communities located near the university. There is an opportunity for universities to teach students and to provide public service by reaching beyond their current geography to forestall news deserts in their states. They could, for example, set up statewide news bureaus that give budding reporters a chance to actually cover regional concerns. A model exists in the now-defunct City News Bureau of Chicago. From the time it was established in the late 19th century until it closed in 2005, it served as a cooperative effort among the city's newspapers to cover breaking news while training new reporters.

**State governments** often provide scholarships to future teachers and doctors to assure an adequate supply in regions of need. In potential news deserts, journalism has reached a point at which scholarships could be devised to supply interns and young reporters to local news organizations. Similarly, the federal government has in the past offered tax incentives for companies that hire people who are unemployed. States could also offer tax incentives for newspapers that hire journalists who cover important public policy issues.

**A dual need exists: to raise awareness in society about the vital role of community news organizations and to hold current newspaper owners accountable for delivering on their civic duty in the digital age.**

**Educators**, as well as many foundations, support media literacy programs. Indeed, the future of democracy depends on students, as emerging voters, comprehending and appreciating the vital role of news media. Some states and communities have had strong newspaper-in-education programs. Unfortunately, they have suffered financially as their sponsoring newspaper companies have cut back. Most of the media literacy programs are now aimed at college students. The fashioning of an informed citizenry depends on both high schools and colleges connecting their students to substantive journalism and teaching their students how to maneuver through the multiple channels of the internet to find comprehensive and credible journalism. The McCormick Foundation, among others, has identified media literacy at the secondary and college level as a major priority in the digital age when "a growing sector of the U.S. population does not distinguish between professional journalists, information spinners and citizen voices. The 24/7 news cycles and digital advances in disseminating information serve to further exacerbate this challenging situation."[125]

**Lawmakers and regulators in Washington** have spent considerable time since the Great Recession of 2008–2009 debating the merits of the big banks and developing stress tests of their financial soundness. At the same time, under the radar, a complex, interrelated and very loosely regulated network of financial institutions has experienced explosive growth. These investment partnerships come in a variety of forms: Some are classic hedge funds or private equity funds. Ironically, anyone who has a pension fund has fueled the rise of these investment groups. Half of the money that has flowed into private equity partnerships has come from the many corporate and public pension fund managers in this country, seeking a higher return than the stock market or other traditional options.[126]

Some of the largest private equity funds are also publicly traded—such as Fortress Investment Group, which is the largest owner of newspapers in the country. Yet their publicly available financial statements and shareholder material offer scant transparency, even as these organizations oversee vast empires that provide services that enhance—or diminish—the quality of life in a community, including hospitals, transportation, emergency call centers, as well as newspapers. With little transparency, there is little way to hold these large corporations accountable, except to their majority investors interested in their own return. Considering the potential impact the financial practices of these investment partnerships could have on communities throughout the country, federal authorities need to turn their attention toward addressing the opaqueness of these organizations—at least as eagerly as they focus on big banks.

In the end, though, **activists and individuals** at the community level may have the most important role to play. Large newspaper companies held by investment entities are even more removed from their communities than the sprawling chains of the late 20th century. Yet communities need strong newspapers. Even though a local newspaper is owned by an investment entity or corporation located somewhere else, it usually has publishers, editors and reporters in the city of publication. Activists and individuals in the community need to insist on coverage of important issues and to deliver criticism of coverage when warranted. In the digital age, person-to-person contact and building relationships continue to matter.

Interviewed in 2013, Charles Broadwell, the fourth-generation family member to serve as publisher of The Fayetteville (North Carolina) Observer, emphasized his paper's longstanding commitment to covering the news not only of Fayetteville and Fort Bragg, but also of all of the 10 counties that encompass the Cape Fear Region in southeastern North Carolina.[127] Eight of the 10 counties are among the poorest and most rural in the state. Even as other newspapers and television stations in Raleigh and Wilmington pulled out in the 1990s, The Observer continued to provide comprehensive and contextual reporting on the major regional and local issues confronting those communities. It was the paper's civic responsibility, he said, to give voice to all the residents in the region, who were tied together socially, politically and, ultimately, economically.

In August 2016, New Media/Gatehouse purchased the 200-year-old Observer from its family owners, who had spent an agonizing year debating this "difficult decision." Commenting on the sale, Gatehouse CEO Kirk Davis noted, "We value the Observer's heritage of delivering rich local content to the Fayetteville metropolitan area, including Fort Bragg."[128] What he did not address is whether the Observer would continue to provide coverage of major issues in the rural, economically struggling counties outside the metro area.

In the coming years, investment entities may yet rise to the challenge and deploy their resources to reinvent local journalism, as well as local advertising. But it will require them to significantly reorient their financial priorities. Instead of a short-term earnings focus, they will need to make a long-term commitment and investment in the civic mission traditionally assumed by newspaper publishers.

One thing is certain: Time is running out. No one interested party—whether individual, institution or newspaper owner—can alone save community journalism. It will take a collaborative effort by many interested parties to meet the challenges posed by changing media ownership during a time of great economic and technological disruption. The fate of local newspapers and communities hangs in the balance.

# SOURCE CITATIONS

1 Alex S. Jones, *Losing the News: The Future of the News That Feeds Democracy*, (Oxford: Oxford University Press, 2011), 4.

2 Laura Owen, "A neighbor is better than a newspaper: A look at local news sources in rural Western mountain communities," *Nieman Lab*, May 19, 2016, http://www.niemanlab.org/2016/05/a-neighbor-is-better-than-a-newspaper-a-look-at-local-news-sources-in-rural-western-mountain-communities/.

3 The Newspaper Association of America, "Newspaper Circulation Volume," March 30, 2015, http://www.naa.org/Trends-and-Numbers/Circulation-Volume/Newspaper-Circulation-Volume.aspx.

4 Pete Chronis, "Saying Goodbye to the Rocky," *The Denver Post*, March 3, 2009, http://www.denverpost.com/2009/03/06/saying-goodbye-to-the-rocky/.

5 Rick Edmonds, "Print Advertising Slump Bites Digitally Oriented Advance too," *Poynter Institute*, July 26, 2015, http://www.poynter.org/2015/print-advertising-slump-bites-digitally-oriented-advance-too/360451/.

6 Andrew Khouri, "Layoffs Hits Freedom Communications as it ceases publication of L.A. Register," *Los Angeles Times*, September 23, 2014, http://www.latimes.com/business/la-fi-la-register-20140922-story.html.

7 Amy Mitchell, Jeffrey Gottfried, Michael Barthel and Elisa Shearer, "The Modern News Consumer," *Pew Research Center Journalism Project RSS*, July 07, 2016, http://www.journalism.org/2016/07/07/the-modern-news-consumer/.

8 Jim Conaghan, Interview with Penny Abernathy discussing digital and print readership, May 02, 2016.

9 "Murdoch's Speech: Full Text," *The Guardian*, April 14, 2005, https://www.theguardian.com/media/2005/apr/14/citynews.newmedia.

10 Mark Perry, "Free-fall: Adjusted for inflation, print newspaper advertising will be lower this year than in 1950," *Carpe Diem Blog*, September 6, 2012, http://mjperry.blogspot.hk/2012/09/freefall-adjusted-for-inflation-print.html.

11 Kathleen Drowne and Patrick Huber, *The 1920s.* (Westport, CT: Greenwood, 2004), 25.

12 Eli Noam, *Media Ownership and Concentration in America*, (Oxford: Oxford UP, 2009), 139.

13 Noam, *Media Ownership and Concentration*, 139-41.

14 Jennifer Saba, "Dealtalk-All the newspapers fit to be sold," *Reuters*, March 25, 2013, http://www.reuters.com/article/newspaper-mergers-idUSL1N0CD82B20130325.

15 Davis Merritt, *Knightfall: Knight Ridder and How the Erosion of Newspaper Journalism Is Putting Democracy at Risk*, (New York: New York AMACOM, 2005), 26-8.

16 Perry, "Free-fall."

17 David Lieberman, "McClatchy to Buy Knight Ridder for $4.5 Billion," *USA TODAY*, March 13, 2006, http://usatoday30.usatoday.com/money/media/2006-03-13-knight-ridder_x.html.

18 Perry, "Free-fall."

19 "CNHI Buys Herald, Allied News," *The Herald, Sharon, Pennsylvania*, February 21, 2002, http://www2.sharonherald.com/localnews/recentnews/0202/ln022102a.html.

20 Jim Kirk, "Hollinger Will Sell Bunch Of Its Papers," *Chicago Tribune*, November 25, 1997, http://articles.chicagotribune.com/1997-11-25/business/9711250339_1_hollinger-international-liberty-group-publishing-leonard-green.

21 "Bradley Family Builds Suburban Kansas City Cluster," *Dirks, Van Essen & Murray*, December 31, 2005, http://www.dirksvanessen.com/articles/view/140/bradley-family-builds-suburban-kansas-city-cluster/.

22 Mark Fitzgerald, "And Then There Were 7: American Community Newspapers Files For Bankruptcy," *Editor & Publisher*, April 28, 2009, http://www.editorandpublisher.com/news/and-then-there-were-7-american-community-newspapers-files-for-bankruptcy/.

23 Noam, *Media Ownership and Concentration*, 6.

24 Jennifer Saba, "Dealtalk-All the newspapers fit to be sold," *Reuters*, March 25, 2013, http://www.reuters.com/article/newspaper-mergers-idUSL1N0CD82B20130325.

25 Jacques Steinberg, "Pulitzer to Be Acquired by Lee Enterprises," *New York Times*, February 1, 2005, http://www.nytimes.com/2005/02/01/business/media/pulitzer-to-be-acquired-by-lee-enterprises.html.

26 "McClatchy Completes Acquisition of Knight Ridder," *McClatchy*, June 27, 2006, http://www.mcclatchy.com/2006/06/27/1629/press-releases.html.

27 Paul La Monica, "News Corp. wins fight for Dow Jones," *CNN Money*, August 3, 2007, http://money.cnn.com/2007/07/31/news/companies/dowjones_newscorp/.

28 Perry, "Free-fall."

29 Alan Mutter, "Newspaper Share Value Fell $64B in '08," January 1, 2009, http://newsosaur.blogspot.com/2008/12/newspaper-share-value-fell-64b-in-08.html.

30  "Debt financing of newspapers in the post-recession era," *Dirks, Van Essen & Murray*, December 31, 2013, http://www.dirksvanessen.com/articles/view/194/debt-financing-of-newspapers-in-the-post-recession-era/.

31  "Fortress Investment Group LLC to Acquire Liberty Group Publishing, Inc. From Leonard Green & Partners, L.P.," *PR Newswire*, May 11, 2005, http://www.prnewswire.com/news-releases/fortress-investment-group-llc-to-acquire-liberty-group-publishing-inc-from-leonard-green--partners-lp-54369852.html.

32  Company Profile: BH Media Group. *Bloomberg*, 2016, http://www.bloomberg.com/profiles/companies/0699245D:US-bh-media-group-inc.

33  Emily Chasan, "MediaNews owner files prepackaged bankruptcy," *Reuters*, January 22, 2010, http://www.reuters.com/article/industry-us-affiliatedmedia-bankruptcy-idUSTRE60M01920100123.

34  Warren Buffett, "2012 Letter to Shareholders," *Berkshire Hathaway*, March 1, 2013, http://www.berkshirehathaway.com/letters/2012ltr.pdf.

35  Warren Buffett, "2014 Letter to Shareholders," *Berkshire Hathaway*, February 27, 2015, http://www.berkshirehathaway.com/letters/2014ltr.pdf.

36  Ben Protess, Jessica Silver-Greenberg and Rachel Abrams, "How Private Equity Found Power and Profit in State Capitols," *NY Times*, July 14, 2016, http://www.nytimes.com/2016/07/15/business/dealbook/private-equity-influence-fortress-investment-group.html?_r=0.

37  "Federal regulation of publicly traded companies," *Reporters Committee for Freedom of the Press*, November 4, 2011, https://www.rcfp.org/sunshine-inc/federal-regulation-publicly-traded-companies.

38  Ibid.

39  (2016) Newcastle Investment Corp., *Who We Are*, accessed August 6, 2016, http://www.newcastleinv.com/about/index.

40  Marie Beaudette, "GateHouse Files for Chapter 11 Bankruptcy Protection," *Wall Street Journal*, September 27, 2013, http://www.wsj.com/articles/SB10001424052702304526204579101353655855062.

41  Jon Chesto, "After Dow Jones deal, Fortress engineers GateHouse bankruptcy and media spin-off," *Boston Business Journal*, September 04, 2013, http://www.bizjournals.com/boston/blog/mass_roundup/2013/09/gatehouse-bankruptcy-and-spinoff.html.

42  Mark Howard, "Flipping newspaper ownership," *Florida Trend*, February 26, 2015, http://www.floridatrend.com/article/18139/flipping-newspaper-ownership.

43  Ibid.

44  Rick Edmonds, "Who is investor Randall Smith and why is he buying up newspaper companies?" *Poynter*, July 27, 2011, http://www.poynter.org/2011/randall-smith-alden-global-capital-newspaper-companies/139962/.

45  Ken Doctor, "What are they thinking? Apollo's acquisition of Digital First Media," *Politico*, March 17, 2015, http://www.politico.com/media/story/2015/03/what-are-they-thinking-apollos-acquisition-of-digital-first-media-003573.

46  Michael Wursthorn, "Newly-Formed Newspaper Company Now 'Less Leveraged' After Consolidation," *Wall Street Journal*, September 14, 2012, http://blogs.wsj.com/privateequity/2012/09/14/newly-formed-newspaper-company-now-less-leveraged-after-consolidation/.

47  "Versa Capital Finalizes Acquisition of The Wet Seal Retail Operations," *Business Wire*, April 15, 2015, http://www.businesswire.com/news/home/20150415006789/en/Versa-Capital-Finalizes-Acquisition-Wet-Seal-Retail.

48  "About Versa Capital Management," Accessed August 06, 2016, https://www.linkedin.com/company/versa-capital-management.

49  "Target Criteria," *Versa Capital Management LLC*, Accessed August 06, 2016, http://www.versa.com/target_criteria.php.

50  Michael Oneal and Steve Mills, "Part One: Zell's Big Gamble," January 13, 2013, http://articles.chicagotribune.com/2013-01-13/business/ct-biz-trib-series-1-20130113_1_sam-zell-randy-michaels-big-gamble

51  "Tribune files for bankruptcy," *NY Times Dealbook*, December 08, 2008, http://dealbook.nytimes.com/2008/12/08/tribune-files-for-bankruptcy/.

52  Robert Channick, "Dold named Chicago Tribune publisher, Ferro donates Sun-Times stake to charitable trust," *Chicago Tribune*, March 02, 2016, http://www.chicagotribune.com/business/ct-tribune-publishing-changes-0303-biz-20160302-story.html.

53  "Tribune Publishing Receives $70.5 Million Growth Capital Investment from Nant Capital," *Business Wire*, May 23, 2016, http://www.businesswire.com/news/home/20160523005650/en/Tribune-Publishing-Receives-70.5-Million-Growth-Capital.

54  "BRK/A: New York stock quote - Berkshire Hathaway Inc.," July 12, 2016, http://www.bloomberg.com/quote/BRK/A:US.

55  Julie Moos, "Media General to sell most of its newspapers to Warren Buffett's Berkshire Hathaway," *Poynter*, May 17,

2012, http://www.poynter.org/2012/media-general-to-sell-most-of-its-newspapers-to-warren-buffetts-group/174282/.

56  Anupreeta Das, "At Papers, Berkshire Rewrites Its Script," *Wall Street Journal*, January 2, 2014, http://www.wsj.com/articles/SB10001424052702304361604579292721064856870.

57  Rem Rieder," Newspapers haven't 'cracked code,' Buffett says," *USA Today*, May 28, 2016, http://www.usatoday.com/story/money/columnist/rieder/2016/05/25/rieder-newspapers-havent-cracked-code-buffett-says/84902818/.

58  Howard Stutz, "Review-Journal, parent Stephens media to be sold to New Media," *Las Vegas Review-Journal*, February 19, 2015, http://www.reviewjournal.com/business/economy/review-journal-parent-stephens-media-be-sold-new-media.

59  "Gannett Board Approves Completion of Spin-off Transaction," *Business Wire*, June 08, 2015, http://www.businesswire.com/news/home/20150608005985/en/Gannett-Board-Approves-Completion-Spin-off-Transaction.

60  Ibid.

61  "Gannett acquires 11 media organizations from Digital First Media," *Gannett*, June 01, 2015, http://www.gannett.com/news/press-releases/2015/6/1/gannett-acquires-11-media-organizations-digital-first-media/.

62  Lisa Beilfuss, "Gannett Buys Assets from North Jersey Media Group," *Wall Street Journal*, July 06, 2016, http://www.wsj.com/articles/gannett-buys-assets-from-north-jersey-media-group-1467836611.

63  Jonathan Lansner, "Digital First closes deal to buy The Orange County Register," *Orange County Register*, March 31, 2016, http://www.ocregister.com/articles/digital-710434-first-register.html.

64  "Digital First Media to Sell the Salt Lake Tribune to Paul Huntsman," *Business Wire*, April 20, 2016, http://www.businesswire.com/news/home/20160420005948/en/Digital-Media-Sell-Salt-Lake-Tribune-Paul.

65  Gerry Smith, "Newspapers Gobble Each Other Up to Survive Digital Apocalypse," *Bloomberg Technology*, March 29, 2016, http://www.bloomberg.com/news/articles/2016-03-29/newspapers-gobble-each-other-up-to-survive-digital-apocalypse.

66  Andrea Chang, "Tribune Publishing completes purchase of U-T San Diego," *Los Angeles Times*, May 21, 2015, http://www.latimes.com/business/la-fi-tribune-san-diego-20150522-story.html.

67  Matthew Ingram, "Tribune Rebuffs Gannett Again, Gets Sued, Changes Name to Tronc," *Fortune*, June 2, 2016 http://fortune.com/2016/06/02/tribune-gannett-tronc/.

68  "Flurry of end of year sales caps off a very active market in 2015 for newspaper transactions," *Inland Press Association*, December 29, 2015, http://www.inlandpress.org/industry/article_f036dc5e-ae4e-11e5-8764-07f17e9e00d1.html.

69  Beau Yarbrough, "Judge halts sale of Register, Press-Enterprise to Tribune Publishing," *Los Angeles Daily News*, March 18, 2016, http://www.dailynews.com/business/20160318/judge-halts-sale-of-register-press-enterprise-to-tribune-publishing.

70  Edmonds, "Print Advertising Slump."

71  "Thirteenth Street Media Managers' Guide," *Scribd*, 2007, https://www.scribd.com/document/221322085/Thirteenth-Street-Media-manager-s-guide.

72  James T. Hamilton, "Subsidizing the Watchdog: What would it Cost to Support Investigative Journalism at a Large Metropolitan Daily Newspaper?" *Duke Conference on Nonprofit Media*, May 4-5, 2009, http://www2.sanford.duke.edu/nonprofitmedia/documents/dwchamiltonfinal.pdf.

73  Rieder, "Rieder: Newspapers haven't 'cracked code.' "

74  Andrew Beaujon, "Warren Buffett expects his papers to deliver 10 percent returns," *Poynter*, May 06, 2013, http://www.poynter.org/2013/buffett-expects-10-percent-return-from-newspapers/212599/.

75  Michael Bush, Gene Hall, Bruce Buchanan, Jeff Brown and Pat Talamantes, "Executive roundtable: Building value in changing times," *Dirks, Van Essen & Murray*, December 31, 2012, http://www.dirksvanessen.com/articles/view/190/executive-roundtable--building-value-in-changing-times/.

76  Ken Doctor, "Newsonomics: Digital First Media's upcoming sale is producing some surprises," *Nieman Lab*, January 15, 2015, http://www.niemanlab.org/2015/01/newsonomics-digital-first-medias-upcoming-sale-is-producing-some-surprises/.

77  James Warren, "Tribune Publishing Combines Editor and Publisher Jobs in Major Shakeup," *Poynter*, March 2, 2016, http://www.poynter.org/2016/tribune-publishing-combines-editor-and-publisher-jobs-in-major-shakeup/399500/.

78  "Thirteenth Street Media Managers' Guide," *Scribd*, 2007, https://www.scribd.com/document/221322085/Thirteenth-Street-Media-manager-s-guide.

79  Brad Badertscher, Dan Givoly, Sharon Katz and Hanna Lee, "Private Ownership and the Cost of Debt: Evidence from the Bond Market," *Columbia Business School*, January 15, 2015, http://papers.ssrn.com/sol3/papers.cfm?abstract_

id=2550300.

80    Jon Chesto, "GateHouse Media's growth bucks the trend," *Boston Globe*, March 11, 2015, https://www. bostonglobe.com/business/2015/03/10/meet-newspaper-industry-biggest-deal-maker/vV6D7uqAo7ssLPaIPk58oL/ story.html.

81    Tanzina Vega, "Online Ambitions, and a Dash of Real Estate, Drive Newspaper Deals," *The New York Times*, January 29, 2012, http://www.nytimes.com/2012/01/30/business/media/online-ambitions-fuel-newspaper-deals.html?_ r=0.

82    "Civitas Media CEO Announces He is Stepping down," *Business Wire*, October 9, 2014, http://www.businesswire. com/news/home/20141009006229/en/Civitas-Media-CEO-Announces-Stepping.

83    "Our Core Values," *Center for News and Design*, http://www.centerfornewsanddesign.com/about-us/.

84    Kristen Hare, "1 year after Project Thunderdome closed, most former staff have pretty great jobs. Here's why," *Poynter*, April 17, 2015, http://www.poynter.org/2015/1-year-after-project-thunderdome-closed-most-former- staff-have-pretty-great-jobs-heres-why/329805/.

85    Michael Barthel, "Newspapers: Fact Sheet," *Pew Research Center*, June 15, 2016, http://www.journalism. org/2016/06/15/newspapers-fact-sheet/.

86    "The 50 State Project," *CQ Roll Call*, July 28, 2015, http://info.cqrollcall.com/rs/764-XAC-282/images/50_State_ Project_2E_FNL2.pdf.

87    Eileen Norcross and Olivia Gonzalez. "Ranking the States by Fiscal Condition," *Mercatus Center at George Mason University*, Arlington, Virginia, March 2015, http://mercatus.org/statefiscalrankings.

88    Chesto, "GateHouse Media's growth."

89    ibid.

90    David Harris, "Gatehouse shakeup forces Boston-area newsroom closure, cuts," *Boston Business Journal*, March 17, 2016, http://www.bizjournals.com/boston/news/2016/03/17/gatehouse-shakeup-forces-boston-area-newsroom. html.

91    Dennis Berman, "Fortress Capital Will Buy Publisher Liberty Group," *Wall Street Journal*, May 11, 2005, http:// www.wsj.com/articles/SB111577592873230054.

92    Robert Channick, "Tribune Publishing completes purchase of Sun-Times suburban properties," *Chicago Tribune*, October 31, 2014, http://www.chicagotribune.com/business/ct-tribune-sun-times-papers-1101-biz-20141030-story. html.

93    Ibid.

94    "The 50 State Project."

95    "GateHouse Completes $380 Million Purchase of Copley Midwest Papers," *Editor & Publisher*, April 11, 2007, http://www.editorandpublisher.com/news/gatehouse-completes-380-million-purchase-of-copley-midwest- papers/.

96    "GateHouse Media officially done with bankruptcy," *Democrat & Chronicle*, November 26, 2013, http://www. democratandchronicle.com/story/money/business/2013/11/26/gatehouse-media-officially-done-with- bankruptcy/3758479/.

97    Tom Knox, "Columbus Dispatch sale finalized; sold for $1 million more than Providence Journal," *Columbus Business First*, June 15, 2015, http://www.bizjournals.com/columbus/news/2015/06/15/columbus-dispatch-sale- finalized-sold-for-1m-more.html.

98    "Brown becomes Ohio Community Media," *Dirks, Van Essen, & Murray*, September 30, 2010, http://www. dirksvanessen.com/articles/view/99/brown-becomes-ohio-community-media/.

99    "The 50 State Project."

100    "Media General Announces Agreements with Berkshire Hathaway for Purchase of Newspapers and New Financing," *Media General*, May 17, 2012, http://www.mediageneral.com/press/2012/may17_12.html.

101    "Halifax Media Group, owner of StarNews, acquired by New Media," *Star News Online*, November 20, 2014, http:// www.starnewsonline.com/news/20141120/halifax-media-group-owner-of-starnews-acquired-by-new-media.

102    "The Fayetteville Observer announces sale."

103    Anupreeta Das, "A Potential Warren Buffett Successor Gets More Duties at Berkshire," *Wall Street Journal*, April 12, 2016, http://www.wsj.com/articles/gen-re-ceo-tad-montross-to-retire-by-year-end-1460475844.

104    "The 50 State Project."

105    Maxwell E. McCombs and Donald L. Shaw, "The Agenda-Setting Function of Mass Media," *Public Opinion Quarterly* 36(2) (1972) 176–187.

106    Jones, *Losing the News*, 4.

107    Steven Waldman, "The Information Needs of Communities: The changing media landscape in a broadband age,"

*Federal Communications Commission*, July 2011, https://transition.fcc.gov/osp/inc-report/The_Information_Needs_of_Communities.pdf.

108    Barthel, "Newspapers: Fact Sheet."

109    Waldman, "The Information Needs of Communities."

110    Martin Kaplan and Matthew Hale, "Local TV News in the Los Angeles Media Market: Are Stations Serving the Public Interest?" *The Norman Lear Center, University of Southern California Annenberg School for Communication & Journalism*, March 11, 2010, https://learcenter.org/pdf/LANews2010.pdf.

111    "2015 Broadband Progress Report," *Federal Communications Commission*, February 04, 2015, https://www.fcc.gov/reports-research/reports/broadband-progress-reports/2015-broadband-progress-report.

112    Amy Mitchell, Mark Jurkowitz, Jesse Holcomb, Jodi Enda and Monica Anderson, "Nonprofit journalism: A Growing but Fragile Part of the U.S. News System," *Pew Research Center*, June 10, 2013, http://www.journalism.org/2013/06/10/nonprofit-journalism/.

113    David Demers, *The Menace of the Corporate Newspaper: Fact or Fiction* (Ames: Iowa State University Press, 1996), 46.

114    Ken Doctor, "The great devaluation of the American daily newspaper," *Politico*, May 19, 2015, http://www.politico.com/media/story/2015/05/the-great-devaluation-of-the-american-daily-newspaper-003784.

115    Walter Lippmann, *Liberty and the News* (New York: Harcourt, Brace and Howe, 1920), 46-7.

116    McCombs and Shaw, "The Agenda-Setting Function."

117    For examples, see research from *Borrell Associates*, https://www.borrellassociates.com/about and Steve Gray, http://snpa.static2.adqic.com/static/2015Summit-Gray.pdf.

118    JoAnn Sciarrino, John Prudente, David Bockino, *In-house Digital Agencies in Community Newspapers: An Adaptive Approach to a Changing Business Environment*, Manuscript submitted for publication, 2016.

119    Steve Gray, "Thought experiments can put us ahead of the media disruption curve," *MediaReset*, June 8, 2016, https://mediareset.com/2016/06/08/thought-experiments-can-put-us-ahead-of-the-media-disruption-curve/.

120    Mary Meeker, "Internet Trends 2016," 2016, via KPCB Code Conference. http://www.kpcb.com/internet-trends

121    Waldman, "The Information Needs of Communities.

122    Emily Le Coz, "Herald-Tribune wins Pulitzer Prize," *Herald-Tribune, Sarasota, Florida*, April 18, 2016, http://www.heraldtribune.com/article/20160418/NEWS/160419628.

123    Susannah Nesmith, "State coverage gets a boost from local-focused media company," *Columbia Journalism Review*, December 09, 2015, http://www.cjr.org/united_states_project/state_coverage_gets_boost_from_local-focused_media_company.php.

124    Anna Clark, "How a new reporting collaborative is building a newsroom that crosses state lines," *Columbia Journalism Review*, March 16, 2016, http://www.cjr.org/united_states_project/ohio_river_network.php

125    "News Literacy," *McCormick Foundation*, accessed August 29, 2016, http://mccormickfoundation.org/democracy/news-literacy.

126    Danielle Ivory, Ben Protess and Kitty Bennett, "When you Dial 911 and Wall Street Answers," *NY Times*, June 25, 2016, http://www.nytimes.com/2016/06/26/business/dealbook/when-you-dial-911-and-wall-street-answers.html.

127    Penelope Muse Abernathy, *Saving Community Journalism: The Path to Profitability*, (Chapel Hill: UNC Press, 2014), 30, 82.

128    "The Fayetteville Observer announces sale."

# METHODOLOGY

This report analyzes data on more than 9,500 daily and weekly papers in the U.S. at three intervals between 2004 and 2016. It draws on statistics in the 2004 and 2014 Editor & Publisher Newspaper Data Book and 2016 E&P data accessed online, in addition to information shared by the consulting firm BIA/Kelsey. Faculty and researchers in the University of North Carolina at Chapel Hill School of Media and Journalism supplemented the information in these databases with extensive reporting and research. They conducted interviews with industry analysts and professionals, and analyzed U.S. Census data, as well as the financial records and press releases issued by newspaper owners.

This report relied initially on analysis of proprietary media statistics compiled by BIA/Kelsey. This was cross-referenced with and supplemented by data from the E&P's 2004 and 2014 Newspaper Data Book, as well as online data accessed June 30, 2016, and merged into the UNC database. This data was then cleaned and updated to reflect recent changes in status for the newspapers in the database.

Both of the large databases we analyzed and used to build the UNC database have the type of reporting errors that are inherent in any survey. Both relied on the accurate feedback of respondents. BIA/Kelsey conducted a telephone survey of newspaper executives and managers while Editor & Publisher employed a digital and mail survey of senior executives at individual papers. When we spotted errors, we corrected them in our database and will continue to update our analysis as new information becomes available. If you detect an error, please fill out and submit the "corrections" form available on our website newspaperownership.com/.

## BUILDING THE DATABASE

Industry representatives and analysts estimate there are 11,000 newspapers in the country. Because the focus of this report is on local news organizations that produce and publish journalism oriented toward a specific geographic region or community, or ethnic group, we excluded the following newspapers and publications from the UNC database and analysis of trends:

- National newspapers: *The New York Times, Wall Street Journal* and *USA Today.*

- Shoppers or similar free advertisement-based works that do not contain local reporting produced by journalists employed by the paper.
- Topic-specific publications such as business journals and lifestyle magazines.
- Newspapers published less than once a week.

As a result of these adjustments, our numbers may differ from those listed on the websites of some companies or in other databases.

In UNC's 2004 database, there are 8,591 local newspapers—6,114 from BIA/Kelsey and 2,477 additional ones from the E&P *Newspaper Data Book* or firsthand research and reporting. In UNC's 2014 database, there are 7,927 newspapers—6,849 from BIA Kelsey and 1,078 from E&P. In UNC's 2016 database, updated to reflect E&P statistics accessed on June 30, 2016, there are 7,863 newspapers.

| | UNC DATABASE | | E&P | | BIA/KELSEY | |
| --- | --- | --- | --- | --- | --- | --- |
| | 2004 | 2014 | 2004 | 2014 | 2004 | 2014 |
| Daily | 1,469 | 1,332 | 1,456 | 1,395 | 1,375 | 1,321 |
| Weekly | 7,122 | 6,595 | 6,704 | 5,710 | 4,749 | 5,571 |
| Total | 8,591 | 7,927 | 8,160 | 7,105 | 6,124 | 6,892 |

Each newspaper entry in the three databases has the following variables: year, name, frequency (daily/weekly), number of days published per week, city, state, parent company and total circulation, as audited by the Alliance for Audited Media (AAM) or reported in other official databases. Each newspaper was then assigned a latitude and longitude, which was used to identify the county where each newspaper was physically located. To be able to identify whether newspapers were located in a rural or an urban area, each was assigned to a corresponding group from the U.S. Department of Agriculture's Rural-Urban Continuum Codes (RUCC) based on the county in which they were located. Additionally, poverty data from each county was merged into the dataset.

The circulation statistics in our database are primarily print-based, an admittedly imperfect measure since they do not count the increasing number of people that access local news online. However, there is currently no widely used and easily accessible tracking system (similar to AAM) that reports online readership data for the wide range of newspapers in this study, especially the thousands of local papers in small and mid-sized markets. Therefore, print circulation is used as a proxy for measuring the decline in both reach and influence of traditional newspapers.

More than a third of the newspapers in our proprietary database changed ownership during the past decade. Increasingly, many dailies are also purchasing small weeklies in adjacent communities. Whenever possible, we attempted to determine parent company for every newspaper—whether corporate or family-owned.

## MEDIA GROUPINGS

Because of the size and complexity of our database, our in-depth analysis of trends focused on the 25 largest companies (in terms of papers owned) in 2004, 2014 and 2016. Between 2004 and 2014, there was extensive turnover in the list of the largest companies.

UNC researchers tracked mergers and acquisitions in the newspaper industry from 2004 to 2016 and assessed corporate strategies by identifying and examining:

- Public corporate documents, including quarterly and annual reports released by the individual companies and by Dirks, Van Essen & Murray, the leading merger and acquisition firm in the U.S. newspaper industry.
- Numerous news articles about individual purchases and business decisions.
- Statements made by executives that were in press

releases, news articles or industry presentations.
- Analytical reports and interviews with industry representatives and analysts.

After extensive reporting and research, each of the largest 25 companies in 2004, 2014 and 2016 was categorized in one of three ways:
- **Private Companies:** This group includes large companies, such as Hearst Corp., which owns a portfolio of media properties, including cable networks and digital enterprises. It also includes the smaller self-described "independent, family-owned companies," such as Boone Newspapers, which owns 74 publications in small and mid-sized communities throughout the South.
- **Public Companies:** These publicly traded entities arose in the latter part of the 20th century and, until recently, were among the largest, in terms of circulation. They include Gannett, Knight Ridder, Lee Enterprises and McClatchy. Most of these companies went public with the stated purpose of raising funds so they could buy other newspapers in attractive high-growth markets.
- **Investment Companies:** This category has arisen in the past decade and has a different ownership philosophy and financial structure from the traditional newspaper owners. It includes privately held entities, such as Community Newspaper Holdings Inc., owned and operated by the Retirement Systems of Alabama, and publicly traded ones, such as New Media/Gatehouse. Companies were classified in this category if they met at least five of the eight characteristics:

### HOW INVESTMENT COMPANIES DIFFER FROM TRADITIONAL NEWSPAPER CHAINS

| CHARACTERISTICS | NewMedia/GateHouse | Digital First | CNHI | Civitas | tronc/Tribune | BH Media | 10/13 Communications |
|---|---|---|---|---|---|---|---|
| The stated emphasis of the parent company is to maximize shareholder return on investment | X | X | X | X | X | X | X |
| Many properties were acquired as a group from other media companies through either purchase of entire companies or divisions. | X | X | X | X | X | X | X |
| Majority financial and/or operational control of the firm is held by a small number of institutional shareholders, such as lenders, private equity firms or investment fund managers. | X | X | X | X | X | | X |
| The company was formed or incorporated within the past two decades and is a relative newcomer to newspaper ownership. | X | X | X | X | | X | |
| The newspaper holdings are part of a portfolio of non-newspaper companies. | X | X | X | X | | X | |
| There has been much movement of individual newspapers within portfolios. | X | X | X | X | X | | |
| There have been two or more financial restructurings, including bankruptcy reorganization, a rebranding after selling the company or flips between public and private ownership. | X | X | X | X | X | | |
| A private equity company, a hedge fund or pension fund has at some point during the past decade owned all or a significant portion of the enterprise. | X | X | X | X | X | | X |

See http://newspaperownership.com/additional-material/ for details on the characteristics of each of the seven largest investment groups.

## MAPPING

The maps in the report provide insights into the rapid growth in the number of investment-owned newspapers and consolidation in the industry. It also suggests areas that may be at risk of losing their prime source of local news—most often the local newspapers—and thus becoming a news desert.

UNC researchers used the data to map the locations of the newspapers as accurately as possible. Both the BIA/Kelsey and E&P 2014 databases incorrectly listed the parent company or city location for many newspapers, especially the smaller ones. UNC researchers attempted to review and correct errors, and then assign the newspaper to the city where it was actually located. There are no street addresses in the UNC database.

## About the BIA/Kelsey Database

BIA/Kelsey, a research and advisory company focused on local advertising and marketing, began tracking newspaper ownership in the United States in 2004. The organization employs a telemarketing team that calls individual newspapers and collects information from employee respondents. The data on local newspapers provided to UNC by BIA/Kelsey included the following: frequency of publication (daily/weekly), number of days published, newspaper name, city and state where newspaper is located, local owner of newspapers, parent company of owner, circulation (daily), circulation (Sunday), circulation (free) and circulation (paid).

## About the Editor & Publisher Database

Editor & Publisher began publishing an annual *Newspaper Data Book* in 1921. The Data Book has information on more than 25,000 companies and more than 160 data fields. Data is collected through mail and email surveys and supplemented by telephone research. Up-to-date data can be accessed online. UNC researchers used *E&P* to supplement and correct incomplete or inaccurate 2004 and 2014 data from BIA/Kelsey. Most recently, E&P's 2016 data, accessed online June 30, 2016, was used to update the information on the individual newspapers in UNC's database.

# ADDITIONAL MATERIAL

Additional information and resources are available at
**http://newspaperownership.com/additional-material/**, including the following:

1. Map locating daily newspapers that were closed or merged, or shifted to weekly publication.

2. List of closed and merged daily newspapers, 2004–2016.

3. List of newspaper owned by the largest 25 companies in 2004, 2014, 2016.

4. Year-by-year timeline of the acquisitions and divestures of the seven largest investment entities.

5. Financial and operational characteristics shared by the seven largest investment entities.

6. Sample of statements made by the executives of the seven largest investment entities.

7. Map locating where the largest 25 companies own newspapers.

8. Map locating where the largest seven investment entities own newspapers.

9. Number of newspapers owned by investment groups in each state.

10. Type of newspapers owned by the largest investment groups (daily and weeklies) and where they are located (rural or metro areas).

11. A list of papers owned by the largest investment groups in these states: Massachusetts, Illinois, Ohio, North Carolina, Kentucky and West Virginia.

# CONTRIBUTORS

*The Rise of a New Media Baron and the Emerging Threat of News Deserts* is produced by the Center for Innovation and Sustainability in Local Media in the School of Media and Journalism at the University of North Carolina at Chapel Hill.

## About the Author
Penelope Muse Abernathy, formerly an executive with the Wall Street Journal and the New York Times, is Knight Chair in Journalism and Digital Media Economics. She is the author of Saving Community Journalism: The Path to Profitability (UNC Press: 2014).

## About the Center
UNC's Center for Innovation and Sustainability in Local Media supports existing and start-up news organizations through its dissemination of applied research and the development of digital tools and solutions. The Center supports the economic and business research of UNC's Knight Chair in Journalism and Digital Media Economics and the Knight Chair in Digital Advertising and Marketing. In addition, it supports professors and students associated with the Reese News Lab, which designs, tests and adapts digital tools for use in small and midsized newsrooms. The Center is funded by grants from the John S. and James L. Knight Foundation and UNC.

## Researchers
- Patrick Sims, Senior Research Associate
- Paula Seligson, Research Assistant, 2014–2016
- Cody Allen, Research Specialist

**Student Researchers include:** Sara Greer (MA '16), Tatiana Quiroga (MA '17), Pressley Baird (MA '16), Justin Blankenship (PhD '16), Laura Marshall (PhD '16), Elise Stevens (PhD '16), Carolina Peterson (BA '14), Jennifer Jordan (BA '15), Andrew Wood (BA '16)

## Other Significant Contributors
- Craig Anderson, Project Director, Center for Innovation and Sustainability in Local Media
- Ferrel Guillory, Professor of the Practice and Co-Founder, EducationNC
- George W. Cloud, Associate Professor of Journalism (Ret.)
- Pamela Evans, Project and Event Coordinator, Center for Innovation and Sustainability
- Joseph Cabosky, Assistant Professor, Public Relations (PhD '15)
- Carol Wolf, Hussman Visiting Lecturer, Business Journalism
- Jiang (John) Gao, Senior Research Associate (2014)
- Allegra L. Jordan, Gold Gable Advisors
- Bruce Kyse, Publisher, Calaveras Enterprise/ Sierra Lodestar

## UNC School of Media and Journalism
www.mj.unc.edu
Susan R. King, Dean

## UNC Center for Innovation and Sustainability in Local Media
www.cislm.org, www.reesenewslab.org
**Professors:**
- Penelope Muse Abernathy, Knight Chair in Journalism and Digital Media Economics
- JoAnn Sciarrino, Knight Chair in Digital Advertising and Marketing
- Ryan Thornburg, Reese Felts Distinguished Professor and Director of the Master's Program
- Steven King, Assistant Professor and Interim Director of the Reese News Lab

## UNC Center for Media Law and Policy
www.medialaw.unc.edu
- Cathy Packer, W. Horace Carter Distinguished Professor and Co-Director
- David Ardia, Assistant Professor, UNC School of Law, Co-Director

CPSIA information can be obtained
at www.ICGtesting.com
Printed in the USA
LVOW06s0248170916

505002LV00004B/6/P